Staff Development Guide for the Parallel Curriculum

Staff Development Guide for the Parallel Curriculum

Cindy A. Strickland | **Kathy Tuchman Glass**

A JOINT PUBLICATION

NATIONAL ASSOCIATION FOR Gifted Children

CORWIN
A SAGE Company

For information:

Corwin
A SAGE Company
2455 Teller Road
Thousand Oaks, California 91320
(800) 233-9936
Fax: (800) 417-2466
www.corwinpress.com

SAGE Ltd.
1 Oliver's Yard
55 City Road
London EC1Y 1SP
United Kingdom

SAGE India Pvt. Ltd.
B 1/I 1 Mohan Cooperative Industrial Area
Mathura Road, New Delhi 110 044
India

SAGE Asia-Pacific Pte. Ltd.
33 Pekin Street #02-01
Far East Square
Singapore 048763

Printed in the United States of America

Library of Congress Cataloging-in-Publication Data

Strickland, Cindy A., 1959-
Staff development guide for the parallel curriculum/Cindy A. Strickland and Kathy Tuchman Glass; A Joint Publication With the National Association for Gifted Children.
    p. cm.
Includes bibliographical references and index.
ISBN 978-1-4129-6380-0 (cloth)
ISBN 978-1-4129-6381-7 (pbk.)

  1. Gifted children—Education—Curricula—Handbooks, manuals, etc. 2. Curriculum planning—Handbooks, manuals, etc. 3. Teachers—In-service training—Handbooks, manuals, etc. I. Glass, Kathy Tuchman. II. Title.

LC3993.2.S87 2009
371.95'3—dc22   2009010941

This book is printed on acid-free paper.

09 10 11 12 13   10 9 8 7 6 5 4 3 2 1

Acquisitions Editor:	David Chao
Editorial Assistant:	Brynn Saito
Production Editor:	Amy Schroller
Copy Editor:	Trey Thoelcke
Typesetter:	C&M Digitals (P) Ltd.
Proofreader:	Charlotte J. Waisner
Indexer:	Jean Casalegno
Cover Designer:	Rose Storey

Contents

About the Authors

Cindy A. Strickland has been a teacher for twenty-five years and has worked with students of all ages, from kindergarten to master's degree. A member of the ASCD Differentiation Faculty Cadre, Cindy works closely with Carol Ann Tomlinson and has coauthored several books and articles with her. In the past eight years, Cindy's consulting work has taken her to forty-six states, five provinces, and three continents where she has provided workshops on topics relating to differentiation, the Parallel Curriculum Model (PCM), and gifted education.

Cindy's publications include *The Parallel Curriculum Model*, 2nd edition; *The Parallel Curriculum Model in the Classroom: Applications Across the Content Areas; Multimedia Kit for the Parallel Curriculum*, a finalist for 2006 Association of Educational Publishers (AEP) Distinguished Achievement Award; and *In Search of the Dream: Designing Schools and Classrooms That Work for High Potential Students From Diverse Cultural Backgrounds.*

Publications in differentiation include *Professional Development for Differentiated Instruction: An ASCD Toolkit, Tools for High-Quality Differentiated Instruction: An ASCD Toolkit,* the ASCD online course *Success With Differentiation,* the book *Differentiation in Practice: A Resource Guide for Differentiating Curriculum, Grades 9–12,* and a unit in the book *Differentiation in Practice: A Resource Guide for Differentiating Curriculum, Grades 5–9.*

Cindy lives in Virginia and can be reached via e-mail at cindy.strickland@gmail.com.

As a former master teacher who holds current teaching certification, **Kathy Tuchman Glass** consults with schools and districts, presents at conferences, and teaches seminars for university and county programs delivering customized professional development. Kathy has been in education for more than twenty years and works with teachers at all levels in groups of varying sizes from one-on-one to entire school districts. She assists administrators and teachers with strategic planning to determine school or district objectives, and she presents and collaborates on designing standards-based differentiated curriculum, crafting essential understandings and guiding questions, using compelling instructional strategies that engage all learners, incorporating various effective assessments into curriculum, using six-trait writing instruction and assessment, creating curriculum maps, and more.

In addition to this work, Kathy has written *Lesson Design for Differentiated Instruction, Grades 4–9, Curriculum Mapping: A Step-by-Step Guide to Creating Curriculum Year Overviews,* and *Curriculum Design for Writing Instruction: Creating Standards-Based Lesson Plans and Rubrics.* In addition, Kathy has served as a reader and reviewer for *Reader's Handbook: A*

Student Guide for Reading and Learning and as a contributing writer and consultant for the Heath Middle Level Literature series.

Originally from Indianapolis, Kathy resides in the San Francisco Bay Area. She can be reached by phone at 650-366-8122 or through her e-mail at kathy@kathyglassconsulting.com. Her Web site can be found at http://www.kathyglassconsulting.com/.

Introduction

FACILITATION GUIDE OBJECTIVES

The purposes of this professional development workbook are to assist teachers and curriculum designers (or teachers themselves) to:

- Understand the purposes, definitions, and driving questions of each of the four parallels comprising the Parallel Curriculum Model (PCM);
- Apply what they have learned to remodel existing curriculum aligned to the characteristics of each parallel using a lesson design template;
- Become familiar with key components of essential curriculum design that serve as the basis for the lesson design template;
- Understand and apply the concept of Ascending Intellectual Demand as included in the lesson template; and,
- Remodel existing curriculum using a combination of parallels to enrich what and how students learn.

In this workbook, you will receive tools, resources, and strategies for accomplishing these things. The work in this guide is based on *The Parallel Curriculum: A Design to Develop High Potential and Challenge High-Ability Learners,* 2nd ed. (2008), developed and written by Carol Ann Tomlinson, Sandra N. Kaplan, Joseph S. Renzulli, Jeanne Purcell, Jann Leppien, Deborah Burns, Cindy Strickland, and Marcia Imbeau. If possible, read that book prior to or in tandem with using this workbook.

The initial chapter of this workbook is devoted to first understanding and exploring the nature and intent of the Parallel Curriculum as a model. It exposes workshop participants to the four parallels, to ways of thinking about course content and the Parallel Curriculum Model. Chapters 2 through 5 delve specifically into each parallel one at a time: Core Curriculum Parallel, Curriculum of Connections, Curriculum of Practice, and Curriculum of Identity. In each chapter, teachers will remodel or design lessons (or units) they currently teach by applying the characteristics of sound PCM lessons within the targeted parallel. Finally, Chapter 6 explores how the four parallels might come together in a single unit to enrich what and how students learn.

COMPONENTS

- The *session overview* provides a brief explanation of what each specific session entails.
- Use the *masters* to make handouts and transparencies as you see fit. The masters are intended to highlight key vocabulary and principles of the PCM and serve as a handy reference for participants as they redesign their own lessons and units.

- The *introduction* sets the stage for the workshop and briefly introduces the topic.

- *Teaching and learning activities* provide an array of material you can use to communicate definitions, characteristics, and concrete examples for components. You determine which mode of presentation (e.g., handouts and/or overheads) works best for you. Participants use the masters, prior knowledge from a previous session, major discussion points, experience, and their materials and resources to redesign or create anew a key component (e.g., assessments, introductory activities, products) of a parallel.

- *Closure/looking forward* provides opportunities for sharing of the work participants accomplished during the teaching and learning activities.

- The timing of a given session will depend on key variables, such as your group size, the expertise of participants, a facilitator's presentation style, and so forth. We suggest that facilitators review all sessions carefully and assign approximate time frames given these variables. Two or more workshop sessions can be combined into a given staff development time allotment. If there is limited time, revise and conduct sessions according to time specifications.

- Scripts are provided in some instances to give you an idea of what we intend to emphasize and our thinking about the topic. Depending on your comfort level, you may use our words verbatim or adapt the language to suit your style. One major goal of this guide is to foster critical thinking and expression during discussion and group interactions so participants are well-versed in the Parallel Curriculum Model and the components of the lesson design template. Therefore discussion questions are interspersed throughout the lessons.

- Appendix A provides *facilitation suggestions* designed to help you lead discussions that foster critical thinking and ground participants in the distinctive and overlapping qualities of the parallels.

- Appendix B provides a game that may be used at any time to assess participant knowledge of basic vocabulary related to the PCM.

- Appendix C lists four key attributes of a Parallel Curriculum unit. This document serves as a final check on whether a unit matches the intents and purposes of this model.

- Appendix D offers the driving questions of the four parallels in one document for reference

- Appendix E provides an overview of the intent and characteristics of the four parallels.

ORGANIZATIONAL SUGGESTIONS

As you proceed from session to session, participants will be accumulating many resources and voraciously creating materials. You might suggest that participants equip themselves with a large three-ring binder that includes tabs. With this—or a similar—organizational system in place, there will be a "home" for the materials they receive and create as you work together.

FEEDBACK

Throughout your work together, you will guide participants in various activities and discussions as they remodel their own lessons and units. Consider to what degree you wish to review the curriculum they design and how you will provide feedback. For example, will you formally provide written feedback for each activity to individual teachers? Will you informally work with teacher groups to share your impressions orally?

Although this workbook was written very carefully to guide you through each step in presenting, you will most assuredly find yourself taking various tangents based on the nature of your group. Give yourself permission to be flexible enough to do that. If you are working alone or with a partner, our intent is that you, too, will find value and guidance for implementing the PCM or pushing your own awareness and expertise to new heights. If you are working with educators that are not in your district, we hope you can create new alliances and relish newfound collegial relationships. Enjoy this experience with your group as you learn and grow together.

Introducing the Parallel Curriculum Model

Note to Facilitator

To prepare for this workshop, you may wish to review Chapter 1, "The Rationale and Guiding Principles for an Evolving Conception of Curriculum" and Chapter 2, "An Overview of the Parallel Curriculum Model" of *The Parallel Curriculum* by Tomlinson, et al., (2008).

Session Overview

This session begins with the belief system on which the Parallel Curriculum Model (PCM) is based and then introduces each of the four parallels.

Masters

- Teaching-Learning Process
- Assumptions Underlying the Parallel Curriculum Model
- The Parallel Curriculum
- Classroom Scenarios

Session Details

Introduction

- Ask participants to define each of the following terms.
  - Curriculum (e.g., what we teach, what we want students to learn)
  - Model (e.g., a structure or design)
  - Curriculum Model (e.g., a format used to design curriculum)

(Continued)

(Continued)

- Distribute "Teaching-Learning Process" and read aloud the definition of curriculum.
- Explain the purpose of studying curriculum models. Ask participants to list curriculum models with which they are already familiar (e.g., Understanding by Design, Success for All) and to say what they have found useful about these models.
- Ascending Intellectual Demand (AID) prompt (an optional discussion prompt for participants already operating at a high level of expertise with respect to curriculum models): Should a curriculum model be adapted in its entirety or is it okay to take bits and pieces from a model and integrate them into your own model? (Most model designers prefer that the model be accepted in its entirety or risk being corrupted. Most teachers prefer to use bits and pieces.)
- Ask participants: Why do we need to think differently about curriculum and instruction today than in the past (e.g., student characteristics, amount of information available, theories of multiple intelligence)?

Say: "The authors of *The Parallel Curriculum* state that all curriculum models are based on a belief system. The Parallel Curriculum Model is based on key beliefs or assumptions."

- Display and distribute "Assumptions Underlying the Parallel Curriculum Model." Ask participants to share their reactions to these assumptions.
  - o What assumptions surprised them? Did not surprise them?
  - o Which are most important to them personally? To their students?
  - o To what degree does their current curriculum offer all students such opportunities?

Say: "What we do and what we ask students to do in the classroom delivers a powerful message about what we believe is most important for learners. Good teachers constantly examine and critique their own practices and beliefs. As we study the Parallel Curriculum Model, it will be our job to uncover evidence that this model adheres to its stated belief system and discuss ways in which we might remodel our own units to better incorporate and/or highlight these beliefs."

Teaching and Learning Activities

- Distribute and/or display "The Parallel Curriculum Model," which provides an overview of each of the parallels.

Say: "The authors of *The Parallel Curriculum* suggest that there are (at least) four parallel ways of thinking about course content. These parallels may be seen as formats through which educators can approach curriculum design in the same subject or discipline. These four parallels comprise the basis for the Parallel Curriculum Model."

- Make the point that each of the parallels has its own unique personality. Ask them what seems familiar and/or unfamiliar about each of these parallels.
- Copy and distribute the sheet titled "Classroom Scenarios." Instruct individuals or small groups to read each scenario presented and try to identify the parallel(s) for which it is written. Encourage participants to explain their thinking. Point out that because the PCM assumes that the Core Curriculum is the basis for all other curriculums, the Core Curriculum is always evident in any combination. Parallels attached to each scenario:
  - o Scenario #1: Curriculum of Connections, Core Curriculum
  - o Scenario #2: Curriculum of Connections, Core Curriculum
  - o Scenario #3: Curriculum of Connections, Core Curriculum
  - o Scenario #4: Curriculum of Practice, Core Curriculum
  - o Scenario #5: Curriculum of Identity, Core Curriculum
  - o Scenario #6: All four parallels
- In small groups or as a whole group, engage in a discussion using questions such as:
  - o What seems to be the difference between the Curriculum of Connections and the Core Curriculum? How are they alike? (Repeat for other parallels.)
  - o Which parallels or aspects of parallels have you experienced as a teacher and/or as a student?

o What would need to change in your curriculum to put it in alignment with one or more of these parallels? What would be the benefits for students? For you?

o How might the PCM help us meet the needs of more students more often?

- If participants worked in small groups, invite each group to share highlights of its discussion.
- Encourage participants to come up with a symbol to represent each of the parallels. This symbol can then be used in their own work to indicate where a particular parallel is employed.

Closure/Looking Forward

- Make the following point clear: "Parallel" should not be taken to mean that the formats or approaches must remain separate and distinct in planning or in classroom use. The PCM assumes that teachers may create appropriately challenging curriculum by using any one parallel or a combination of parallels as a framework for thinking about and planning curriculum as shown in the various scenarios.

Say: "If a unit is to be a Parallel Curriculum unit, not only the unit, but all of its component parts must reflect the intent and purposes of the model as a whole or one of its parallels. In the next workshop, we will identify and examine these key components of curriculum."

TEACHING-LEARNING PROCESS

The field of education often uses the term *curriculum* or *curriculum and instruction* to refer to the *purposeful, proactive organization, sequencing, and managing of . . . interactions* across . . . three classroom elements: the *content, the teacher, and the student.* The curriculum, then, is a multifaceted plan that fosters these connections (Tomlinson, et al., 2008, p. 41).

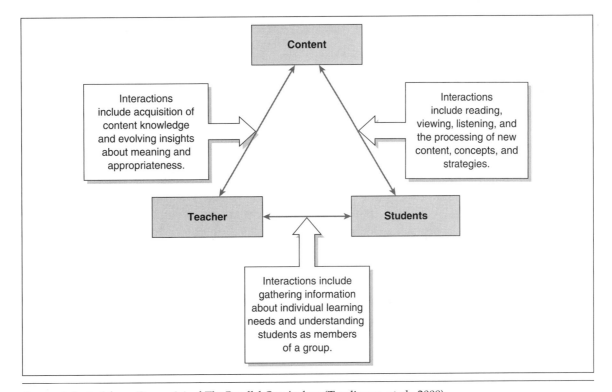

Source: Adapted from Figure 3.1 of *The Parallel Curriculum* (Tomlinson, et al., 2008).

ASSUMPTIONS UNDERLYING THE PARALLEL CURRICULUM MODEL

Curriculum should

- Guide students in mastering key information, ideas, and the fundamental skills of the disciplines.
- Help students grapple with complex and ambiguous issues and problems.
- Guide students in progressing from novice toward expert levels of performance in various subject areas.
- Provide students opportunities for original, creative, and practical work in the disciplines.
- Help students encounter, accept, and embrace challenge.
- Help students uncover, recognize, and apply the significant and essential concepts and principles in each subject area that explain the structure and workings of the discipline, human behavior, and our physical world.
- Help students develop a sense of themselves as well as of their possibilities in the world in which they live.
- Be compelling and satisfying enough to encourage students to persist despite frustration and understand the importance of effort and collaboration.

Source: Adapted from *The Parallel Curriculum* (Tomlinson, et al., 2008, p. 3).

THE PARALLEL CURRICULUM

The Core Curriculum

This parallel reflects the essential nature of a discipline as experts in that discipline conceive and practice the discipline. It is the foundational curriculum that establishes a rich framework of a discipline's key information, skills, concepts, and principles. It is the starting point for all of the parallels in this model.

The Curriculum of Connections

This parallel expands on the Core Curriculum by guiding students to make connections of key concepts and principles within or across disciplines, across times, across cultures or places, or in some combination of those elements.

The Curriculum of Practice

This parallel guides learners in understanding and applying the facts, concepts, principles, and methodologies of the discipline in ways that encourage student growth toward expertise in the discipline. Its purpose is to help students function with increasing skill and confidence in a discipline as professionals and scholars would function.

The Curriculum of Identity

Curriculum developed according to this parallel guides students in coming to understand their own strengths, preferences, values, and commitment by using the key concepts, principles, and skills of contributors and professionals in a field of study. The goal of this parallel is to help students gain a better understanding of both the discipline and themselves.

Adapted from *The Parallel Curriculum* (Tomlinson, et al., 2008) Figures 2.2 to 2.5.

CLASSROOM SCENARIOS

Directions: Read each scenario. Then, match each scenario to the parallel or parallels it seems to reflect: (1) the Core Curriculum; (2) the Curriculum of Connections; (3) the Curriculum of Practice; and/or (4) the Curriculum of Identity. Be ready to explain your thinking.

Scenario #1

After a study of the American Revolution, Mrs. Yee's students scanned a collection of major national newspapers and news magazines for the purpose of identifying contemporary revolutions. Next, students classified their examples as social, political, or economic revolutions. With the teacher's guidance, students then conducted a comparative analysis of the origin and effects of the contemporary revolutions and the American Revolution.

The final outcome defined for the learning experience was for students to apply their discipline-related knowledge and understanding to a present-day conflict. The essential question guiding student work was "How can knowledge of the American Revolution be used to help us understand and respond to revolution in today's world?" Students selected from a variety of contemporary revolutions to which they applied insights about causes of, reactions to, and effects of the American Revolution as a means of thinking about causes of, reactions to, and potential effects of a contemporary cultural change.

Scenario #2

In Mrs. Bernstein's middle school history class, making connections is an ongoing emphasis for all students. Throughout the year, three concepts are used to organize the curriculum: culture, continuity, and diversity. At the end of the second quarter, all students will work with projects that ask them to use these concepts to compare their own culture with that of Russia. Many students will select or develop a family that is similar to theirs but that lives in Russia. The students will then select or develop ways to show how the geography in which the two families live is alike and different. They'll also show how music, technology, religion, and jobs have changed for their own family and for the Russian family in the past twenty-five years. In the end, they'll write about ways in which continuity and diversity are evident in the two cultures over the past two-and-a-half decades. Additionally, each student keeps a journal that relates the three concepts of culture, continuity, and diversity to (1) what students are studying in other classes and (2) the world around them (e.g., music, home, current events, movies, reading).

Scenario #3

Ms. Lance wants to organize and extend expectations for teaching and learning the district's standards. For example, science standards direct that students study living things in their environment. She and her students use the concepts of change and interaction to further organize, explain, clarify, and exemplify the standard. Two of the key principles she introduces are "Change is a result of interactions" and "Interactions can result in change." Her students will take part in an ongoing "mental treasure hunt" to look for evidence within their study of living things that supports these principles. The teacher will use a large wall chart to display student examples and evidence from their study and research. As the year progresses, Ms. Lance will use a second chart to record examples and evidence of the same principles at work in other science topics the students study. The framework also will be useful to guide the work of students who do extended readings in science on topics in which they have particular interest or skill.

Scenario #4

Ms. Harrington's students always work on a long-term, real-world problem as a part of the middle school curriculum that introduces skills and concepts of algebra and geometry. Participation in the problem-solving project also helps students extend and apply previously learned skills in the basic mathematical operations. This year, students will study a traffic problem that became evident at the construction site for a new high school down the highway from their middle school. Working with this problem, the students will function as traffic engineers and use a variety of math skills that draw on their various mathematical strengths and interests. Some of their work will involve collaboration with architects and highway engineers, careful examination of the high school site, data collection, and assessment of the situation.

Scenario #5

In Ms. Mitchell's eleventh grade English class, writing is a centerpiece of the curriculum. All students work to meet certain prescribed writing standards, and all students regularly take part in writing workshops. Students also select a kind of writing for further exploration. Amy selected a genre in which she has a personal interest—short stories and novels. She will address the overarching question, "What does it mean to be a writer?" by studying writers in depth, relevant to her preferred genre. Her reflections will be crafted in her chosen genre. Ultimately, she should have a fuller sense of what it means for others to be writers, but also ways in which the pursuit of writing is (or is not) a good match for her own interests, habits, and perspectives. Amy should also develop insights into ways in which the pursuit of writing might contribute to her own life and ways in which she might contribute to the writing field.

Scenario #6

Beth, a fifth grade student, had a strong ability in reading, thinking, and research. She worked on a special project that began with the concept of "interconnectedness" as it related to the Civil War. In her small town, she discovered a cemetery containing several graves of young women about her age, all of whom died during the Civil War. She pursued the question "In what ways were the lives of young people affected by the Civil War?" As a result, she found an interconnection between disease and the Civil War.

Beth used primary documents at the local courthouse to investigate the young people's graves. Later, she found relatives of the young women still living in her area. Through interviews with these relatives, experts on the Civil War, additional primary documents, and numerous secondary sources, she reconstructed events that dominated the lives of the young women.

She presented her findings in a formal paper to the local historical society where she received encouragement for her work and suggestions for next steps she might take. As her research continued, she translated her findings to a work of historical fiction that she created reflecting the lives of the young women in the graveyard—meeting regularly with professional writers who held scheduled meetings to discuss her work. In the final chapter of her book, she posed discussion questions that might be used in a classroom or book club setting to help teachers or facilitators engage readers in further introspection of her work. Several questions asked readers to make connections, for example: *What were the affects of various wars on young people throughout time and across cultures (e.g., World War II—minority children as victims of the Holocaust and Nazi children; American Revolution—patriots' children and Tories' children)?*

Beth's story was published, as was a reflective piece on a journal she kept throughout the year that captured what she had learned about herself as she worked like a historian and then like a writer of historical fiction. This reflective journal helped Beth to become much more aware of who she was and what she valued through her experiences on this project.

Note: Scenarios #1 through #5 are adapted from *The Parallel Curriculum* (Tomlinson, et al., 2002); Scenario #6 is adapted from the second edition (Tomlinson, et al., 2008).

WORKSHOP #2

The Role of Concepts and Principles in the Parallel Curriculum Model

---

Note to Facilitator

To prepare for this workshop, you may wish to review Chapter 3 of *The Parallel Curriculum*, "Thinking About the Elements of Curriculum Design" (Tomlinson, et al., 2008). Additional background information may be found in *Understanding by Design* by Grant Wiggins and Jay McTighe (1998) and *Concept-Based Curriculum and Instruction: Teaching Beyond the Facts* by H. Lynn Erickson (2002).

Session Overview

This session introduces eleven components of curriculum design that will form the basis of participants' work with each of the parallels. Because of their importance to the PCM, the session places an emphasis on helping participants gain or refine their understanding of the role of concepts and principles in curriculum design, aspects of the content component.

Masters

- Key Components of Comprehensive Curriculum
- Concepts and Principles
- From Concepts to Principles
- A Comparison of Discipline-Based Concepts With Interdisciplinary Macroconcepts
- Component Jigsaw

Session Details

Introduction

Say: "*The Parallel Curriculum* authors remind us that there is no one right way to design curriculum. There are, however, a number of elements that many curriculum designers address during the process of writing a unit. As we remodel existing curriculum or write new curriculum based on this model, we will pay attention to eleven separate, yet interrelated elements."

- Show "Key Components of Comprehensive Curriculum." Assign pairs or small groups of teachers to one or more components and ask them to define their assigned component(s) and give an example of what the component would look like in their own curriculum.
- Distribute "Key Components of Comprehensive Curriculum" and compare the authors' thoughts to those of participants. Tell participants not to worry about what *AID* refers to—you will explore that concept in later sessions. For now, just tell them it is a kind of differentiation.

(Continued)

(Continued)

Teaching and Learning Activities

Say: "A distinguishing feature of the PCM is that its curriculum is firmly rooted in the key concepts and principles of a discipline. In a PCM unit, these aspects of the content component are consistently reinforced to maximize learning and retention. They remain in the forefront of every unit and are adapted to match the intent and purposes of the particular parallel(s) upon which a unit is based. In order to design and remodel units that fit the PCM, teachers must therefore have a clear understanding of these terms."

Note to Facilitator

It is vital that participants be able to identify and incorporate concepts and principles into their unit designs. Based on participants' background knowledge and comfort level with these terms, choose one or both of the following activities to help participants gain and refine their understanding of concepts and principles:

Concepts and Principles: Novice Level

- On the whiteboard or overhead, make a two-column chart. Label one column "in" and the other column "out." It will look like this:

IN	OUT

- Lead a game in which you enter words in the "out" column that are *not* concepts and enter words in the "in" column that *are* concepts. Enter words one at a time and pause after each entry to ask participants: "What is the rule that accounts for the entries in the 'in' column? In other words, what do all the entries in the 'in' column have in common?"

- Here are concepts that you might enter in the "in" column: *culture, systems, interdependence, change, adaptation, migration, function, patterns, conflict.* For the "out" column, you might enter any words that are not concepts, such as: *mousepad, Periodic Table, telephone, enjoyment, sisters, American Revolution, animals, Crusades, screen.* Enter as many line items as it takes for participants to guess what the "in" column words have in common.

- Once participants have identified an appropriate rule for identifying concepts, explain that principles state the relationship between two or more concepts. For example: ask participants to identify and underline the concepts in each of the statements below.

  ○ *Conflicts* arise between *protagonists* and *antagonists.*
  ○ Two positive *numbers* can be added in either *order.*
  ○ *Cultures* have *rules* to provide an orderly existence.
  ○ Members of a *culture* have established *roles.*
  ○ *Folktales* are a means of sharing religious *beliefs* and *customs.*
  ○ *Friendship* involves *cooperation.*
  ○ *Change* may create *conflict.*
  ○ Distribute "Concepts and Principles." Ask them to work alone or with one or two others to give examples of concepts and principles from their own disciplines.
  ○ Distribute "A Comparison of Discipline-Based Concepts With Interdisciplinary Macroconcepts" for future reference.

Concepts and Principles: Intermediate Level

- Display "From Concepts to Principles." Ask participants to formulate principles by showing the relationships between two concepts. To do this, they choose concepts from the first column of the handout and use the verbs in the other columns to show relationships. Note that it may be necessary to vary the form of the verb and/or add prepositions for the principle statements to make sense.
- Ask participants to sit in subject-alike groups. Instruct participants to agree on one unit of study that they all teach and identify any content standards associated with the unit.
- Remind participants that some standards have concepts and principles embedded within them. Others refer only to knowledge and/or skills that are (or should be) associated with key concepts and principles. Encourage participants to uncover and identify the key concept(s) and principle(s) in their standards. "A Comparison of Discipline-Based Concepts With Interdisciplinary Macroconcepts" may be helpful in their work.
- If they need an example, share the following fifth grade California social studies content standard examples or examples from your standards documents.
  - Trace the routes of the major land explorers of the United States, the distances traveled by explorers, and the Atlantic trade routes that linked Africa, the West Indies, the British colonies, and Europe. (Possible concepts: exploration, trade. Possible principle: exploration increases opportunities for trade among disparate peoples.)
  - Describe the competition among the English, French, Spanish, Dutch, and Indian nations for control of North America. (Possible concepts: nation, conflict. Possible principle: nations compete for resources and power, oftentimes leading to conflict among peoples.)
- Lead a discussion about the value of using concepts and principles to guide a unit of study as opposed to the topics and details listed in many content standards.

Note to Facilitator

Because an understanding of concepts and principles is so integral to this model, we have chosen to focus this workshop on that aspect of content. If you have the time or the need to further investigate some or all of the identified components of curriculum, assign appropriate jigsaw readings from *The Parallel Curriculum*, second edition, pages 41–60. Each teacher or group of teachers could read and become "experts" in one or two components and then share their expertise with those who examined the other targeted components. See "Component Jigsaw" for detailed instructions.

Closure/Looking Forward

Say: "Throughout our work with the parallels, we will focus on ensuring that concepts and principles remain at the forefront of our own and our students' thinking. The following series of workshops will help us examine each of the parallels in more depth. In each session, you will have the opportunity to remodel or design one or more curriculum components to match the intents and purposes of a specific parallel."

Note to Facilitator

In the following workshops, teachers will remodel lessons or a unit they currently teach by applying the characteristics of sound PCM lessons. It may be appropriate for participants to bring the following: (1) district or state standards, curriculum guides, benchmarks, and so on; (2) lesson(s) or unit to be remodeled; (3) materials and resources for the lesson(s) or unit; and, (4) laptops (if they are in the habit of using them).

KEY COMPONENTS OF COMPREHENSIVE CURRICULUM

- Content (including standards)
- Assessments
- Introductory Activities
- Teaching Strategies
- Learning Activities
- Grouping Strategies
- Resources
- Products
- Extension Activities
- Differentiation Based on Learner Need (including AID)
- Lesson and Unit Closure

KEY COMPONENTS OF COMPREHENSIVE CURRICULUM

	Definitions	*Exemplary Characteristics*
Content (Including Standards)	• What we want students to know, understand, and do as a result of teaching and learning. • Often written as objectives, grade-level expectations, or as broad K–12 standards statements.	• Incorporate concepts, enduring understandings, and the processes and skills used within a discipline. • Provide clarity, power, and authenticity for teachers and students.
Assessments	• Varied tools and techniques that teachers use to determine students' prior knowledge or the extent to which students are learning and applying content goals. • Used to make instructional decisions.	• Diagnostic, aligned with the learning goals, provide a high ceiling, as well as a low baseline, to ensure that all students' learning can be measured. • Used before, during, and after instruction. • Inform instruction.

Introductory Activities	• Sets the stage for a unit.
	• Components may include:
	  ○ A focusing question;
	  ○ An assessment to determine students' prior knowledge, interests, and learning preferences;
	  ○ A teaser or "hook" to motivate students;
	  ○ Information about the real-world relevance of the goals and unit expectations;
	  ○ Information about expectations for students; and
	  ○ Consideration of students' interests in or experiences that connect with the unit topic.
		• Includes many or most of these six elements, as well as an advance organizer that provides students with information that they can use to help assess their acquisition of the unit's learning goals.

Teaching Strategies	• Methods teachers use to support student learning. • Help teachers introduce, explain, demonstrate, model, coach, guide, transfer, or assess learning.	• Closely aligned to research, learning goals, and learner characteristics. • Varied, promote student involvement, and provide support and feedback.
Learning Activities	• Cognitive experiences that help students perceive, process, rehearse, store, and transfer knowledge, understanding, and skills.	• Aligned with the learning goals and efficiently foster cognitive engagement (e.g., analytic, critical, practical, and creative thinking) integrated with the learning goal.
Grouping Strategies	• Varied approaches a teacher can use to arrange students for effective learning in the classroom.	• Aligned with the learning goals. • Varied and change frequently to accommodate students' interests, questions, learning preferences, prior knowledge, learning rate, and zone of proximal development. • Group membership may change frequently.

	Definitions	*Exemplary Characteristics*
Resources	• Materials that support learning during the teaching and learning activities	• Varied in format. • Link closely to the learning goals, students' reading and comprehension levels, and learning preferences.
Products	• Performances or work samples created by students that provide evidence for student learning. • Represent daily or short-term student learning, or provide longer-term, culminating evidence of student knowledge, understanding, and skill.	• Authentic, equitable, respectful, efficient, aligned to standards, and diagnostic. • Often double as assessment tools.
Extension Activities	• Preplanned or serendipitous experiences that emerge from learning goals, local events, and students' interests.	• Provide for student choice. • Relate to the content/standards, are open ended, are authentic, and generate excitement for and investment in learning.
Differentiation Based on Learner Need (Including AID)	• Optimize the match between the curriculum and students' unique learning needs. (One kind of modification represented in the Parallel Curriculum Model is referred to as Ascending Intellectual Demand).	• Closely aligned with the learning goals, research, assessment data, students' prior knowledge, cognitive skills, motivation, interests, learning modes, questions, and product preferences.

Lesson and Unit Closure	• Allows for reflection on the "punch line" of the lesson.
	• Answers questions such as:
	  ○ What was the point of the lesson?
	  ○ What are students taking away from it?
	  ○ What questions remain?
	  ○ What comes next?
		• Helps students focus on what matters most.
		• Makes explicit ideas that may have been less clear to students during the unit or lesson.

CONCEPTS AND PRINCIPLES

	Definition	*Examples*
CONCEPTS	• Concepts are typically expressed in one word (e.g., *pattern, change, system*), but they can also be expressed by a phrase that acts as one word (e.g., *checks and balances*). • There are subject-specific concepts; for example, *adaptability, organism* for the study of science or *civilization, geography* for the study of social studies. There are also generic or macroconcepts that cut across all disciplines, such as *change, interdependence, movement, system*. • A concept is a general idea or understanding, generalized idea of a thing or a class of things, a category or classification.	• Pattern • Change • System • Movement • Interdependence • Biome • Add your own examples:

(Continued)

(Continued)

	Definition	Examples
PRINCIPLES	• Principles may be described as fundamental truths, laws, rules, or doctrines that explain the relationship between two or more concepts. • Once again, principles may be discipline specific or transcend disciplines.	(Concepts underlined) • <u>Balance</u> is an important factor in predicting the longevity of a <u>biome</u>. • Forms of <u>government</u> allow for varying amounts of individual <u>freedom</u>. • An artist's use of <u>light</u> changes the rendering of a <u>landscape</u>. • *Conflicts* arise between <u>protagonists</u> and <u>antagonists</u>. • <u>Cultures</u> have <u>rules</u> to provide an orderly existence. • Two positive <u>numbers</u> can be added in either <u>order</u>. • Add your own examples: _____ _____ _____ _____ _____

Source: Adapted from *The Parallel Curriculum* (Tomlinson, et al., 2008) Figure 4.3.

FROM CONCEPTS TO PRINCIPLES

Concepts	Verbs	
Form Function Systems Structure Change Movement Perspective Communities Adaptation Survival Traditions Interdependence Conflict Patterns	• is • are • is . . . to • are . . . to • must • might • must have • might have • may be • might be • has • have	• cause(s) • provide(s) • involve(s) • correlate(s) • consider(s) • reflect(s) • satisfy(ies) • follow(s) • learn(ed) • connect(ed) • consider(ed)

A COMPARISON OF DISCIPLINE-BASED CONCEPTS WITH INTERDISCIPLINARY MACROCONCEPTS

Social Studies Concepts	Science Concepts	Art Concepts	Music Concepts
transportation	evaporation	shadow	scales
government	circulation	light	notation
tributary	fertilization	perspective	rhythm
war	temperature	depth	beat
battle	gravity	hue	percussion
treaty	magnetism	tint	woodwind
commerce	energy	composition	harmony
leader	work	texture	echo
services	matter	line	jazz
goods	homeostasis	dimensionality	timbre
resources	sound	symmetry	resonance
culture	waves	portrait	range
immigration	resonance	media	baritone
poverty	plasticity	abstract	projection
navy	scientific	method	gradiant
explorer	evidence	aesthetic	mood
delta	migration	landscape	pitch
caste	tropism	realism	volume
migration	movement	influence	melody
longitude	pressure	balance	conductor
Language Arts	Health and Physical Education Concepts	Interdisciplinary Macroconcepts	Math Concepts
vowel	touchdown	multiplication	form
stereotype	goal	sum	function
claim	heatstroke	integer	systems
persuasion	dribble	prime number	structure

(Continued)

(Continued)

Language Arts	Health and Physical Education Concepts	Interdisciplinary Macroconcepts	Math Concepts
hero	drug	ratio	change
conflict	linesman	angles	communities
folktale	cancer	mode	constancy
resolution	fluid	denominations	symbolism
poetry	sprint	symbols	relationships
alliteration	fullback	ray	properties
symbols	sunscreen	perimeter	measurement
syllable	referee	correlation	classes
noun	offense	standard	deviation patterns
preposition	antioxidant	central	tendency
personification	warm-up	order of operations	cycles
skim	point guard	graph	variables
point of view	protein	pie chart	factors
cause and effect	emergency	random	criticism
archetype	accident	symmetry	movement
main idea	conditioning	chaos	perspective

Adapted from *The Parallel Curriculum* (Tomlinson, et al., 2002) Figure 5.5.

COMPONENT JIGSAW

Read

Read your assigned section(s) in *The Parallel Curriculum*. As you read, highlight key points and jot down any questions you have. Be sure you can do the following.

- Provide a definition of the component(s) in your own words.
- Share what the component(s) would look like in your own or another discipline.
- Explain why the component(s) should be included in unit plans. Consider: Is the component "nice to have" or is it imperative? What would happen if the component were not included?

Discuss

Share your thoughts, questions, and examples with others assigned to the same section(s). Be sure you are all in agreement about the component's role in curriculum design.

Share

Regroup so that experts from each of the eleven components are represented in your new group. Take turns teaching the others about your assigned component(s).

Speculate

- How important is it that every unit of study pays attention to each of the eleven components?
- Which components are consistently a part of your own unit design? Which components do you wish to address more fully?
- Consider the four parallels of the PCM: Core, Connections, Practice, Identity. How might the components vary in units devoted to each of the parallels?

The Core Curriculum Parallel

The Core Curriculum Parallel

Note to Facilitator

To prepare for the workshops in this chapter, you may wish to review Chapter 3, "Thinking About the Elements of Curriculum Design," and Chapter 4, "The Core Curriculum Parallel," of *The Parallel Curriculum* (Tomlinson, et al., 2008).

Session Overview

This session focuses on the definition, intent, benefits, and driving questions of the Core Curriculum Parallel.

Masters

- Nuts and Bolts of the Core Curriculum Parallel
- Core Curriculum at Work in the Classroom
- Checklist for Designing Curriculum Within the Core Curriculum Parallel

Session Details

Introduction

Ask participants to share what comes to mind when they hear the word *core*.

Ask: "Now pair the word *core* with the word *curriculum*. How would you define a *core curriculum*?"

Teaching and Learning Activities

- Distribute "Nuts and Bolts of the Core Curriculum"

Say: "The Core Curriculum is the foundational curriculum that should establish for students a rich framework of the knowledge, understanding, and skills most relevant to the discipline. It's inclusive of and extends state and district expectations. It's the starting point or root system for all effective curriculums including each of the other parallels in this model."

- Ask participants to think about a topic within their curriculum and consider what makes that topic central to a study of their discipline. Suggest they use the "Driving Questions of the Core Curriculum" to help them examine this topic. If they decide a particular topic is not a good example of core knowledge, understanding, and skills, ask them to consider other topics that might better represent the discipline.
- Distribute "Core Curriculum at Work in the Classroom." Work together or in small groups to discuss ways in which these examples match the intent and purposes of the Core Curriculum and address its driving questions.
- Ask participants to examine an existing unit from their own or their district's curriculum that is quite familiar to them. Distribute "Checklist for Designing Curriculum Within the Core Curriculum Parallel" and ask them to use this checklist to compare the degree to which the unit includes key attributes of a Core Curriculum unit.

Closure/Looking Forward

- In small groups and then whole group sharing, invite participants to make a list of the benefits that the Core Curriculum can offer teachers and students.
- Tell participants that the next series of workshops will focus on examining what the key components of curriculum might look in a Core Curriculum unit.
- Remind them of the symbol they developed in Workshop #1 to represent the Core Curriculum. Ask them if they wish to change or adapt this symbol now that they have more information about this parallel.

NUTS AND BOLTS OF THE CORE CURRICULUM PARALLEL

Intents/Purposes of the Core Curriculum

- Provides a format and set of procedures to get to the core, fundamental, or essential knowledge, meaning, and structure of a discipline as topics in that discipline are taught.
- Helps teachers and curriculum designers focus on knowledge that transcends a topic and links learners to the very core of the discipline, enabling students to use their knowledge of one topic to understand the overarching structure of an entire discipline.
- Directly promotes students' proficiency, skillfulness, independence, and self-efficacy in the discipline, thus promoting movement toward expertise.

Driving Questions of the Core Curriculum

- What does this information mean?
- Why does this information matter?
- How is this information organized to help people use it better?
- How and why do these ideas make sense?
- What are these ideas and skills for?
- How do these ideas and skills work?
- How can I use these ideas and skills?

Adapted from *The Parallel Curriculum* (Tomlinson, et al., 2008) Figure 4.1.

CORE CURRICULUM AT WORK IN THE CLASSROOM

Secondary Example

Ms. Berkett, a middle school language arts teacher, wants to organize and extend expectations for teaching and learning the district's standards. Specifically she is focusing on the study of literature and defining characteristics of fiction. She and her students use the concepts of plot, theme, and other elements of literature to further explain, clarify, and exemplify the standard. Two of the key principles she introduces are "Theme represents the author's message and main idea of the work" and "Readers can agree on plot events that take place, but have differing views on theme." Her students will read various works of literature and discuss these principles. Students will create graphic organizers to record examples and evidence of elements of literature from a collection of works. As the year goes on, Ms. Berkett's students will add to these graphic organizers to record additional examples and evidence of the same principles at work in other literature (e.g.., short stories, novels) the students study.

Elementary Example

Topic	Fairy Tales
Discipline	Language Arts

Facts	• A fairy tale is a story handed down from generation to generation.
	• Eight elements are common to all fairy tales:
	  1. The beginning of a fairy tale starts with "Once upon a time . . . " or a similar phrase.
	  2. Magical events, characters, and objects are part of the story.
	  3. One character is someone of royalty, like a king, queen, prince, or princess.
	  4. One character is wicked or evil.
	  5. One character is good.
	  6. Goodness is rewarded in the story.
	  7. Certain numbers like three or seven are in the story; for example, three little pigs or seven fairies.
	  8. The story ends with " . . . and they lived happily ever after" or a similar phrase.

Concepts	• Hero (Protagonist) • Main Idea (Theme) • Conflict (Problem)
Principles	• A basic fairy tale theme is good versus evil. • Conflicts arise between protagonists and antagonists.
Skills	• Summarize; reread (i.e., reading comprehension strategies) • Brainstorm, structure a paper, edit, revise (i.e., writing strategies) • Compare/contrast
Applications (Learning Activities)	• Retell a fairy tale. • Create a fairy tale on paper or orally. • Apply knowledge of good-versus-evil theme to other stories. • Compare and contrast different versions of the same fairy tale. • Identify conflicts between protagonist and antagonist.

Adapted from *The Parallel Curriculum* (Tomlinson, et al., 2008) pp. 85–86.

CHECKLIST FOR DESIGNING CURRICULUM WITHIN THE CORE CURRICULUM PARALLEL

To what degree:

- Is the unit built on key facts, concepts, principles, and skills essential to the discipline?
- Is the unit coherent in its organization?
- Is the unit purposefully focused and organized to achieve essential outcomes (including standards)?
- Does the unit promote understanding rather than rote learning?
- Is the unit taught in a meaningful context?
- Does the unit cause students to grapple with ideas and questions, using both critical and creative thinking?
- Is the unit mentally and affectively engaging and satisfying to learners?
- Does the unit result in evidence of worthwhile student production?

Adapted from *The Parallel Curriculum* (Tomlinson, et al., 2008) Figure 2.1.

WORKSHOP #4

Content Component of a Core Curriculum Unit

Session Overview

In this workshop, participants will examine what the content component of curriculum should look like in a Core Curriculum unit. They also will work to design or revise their own unit content to match the intent and purposes of this parallel.

Masters

- Content
- Matching Content to Core

Session Details

Introduction

If necessary, review "Key Components of Comprehensive Curriculum" (Workshop #2)

Say: "Strong, effective units include most or all of the key components. As we approach each parallel, however, you will notice how the components take on a slightly different flavor. Although we will examine each component one at a time and in a specific order, remember that the components are not necessarily visited in sequence. Rather, most curriculum writing is a recursive process, full of fits and starts and refashioning."

Teaching and Learning Activities

- Remind participants of the work you did with concepts and principles in Workshop #2. Tell them that the *content* of a unit can also refer to the discipline-related facts, skills, and attitudes that we want students to obtain.

(Continued)

(Continued)

Distribute "Content." Briefly go over the definition and characteristics of the content component. Explain that one way to look at content is to subdivide it into categories of knowledge. Ask them to study the examples given for each category of knowledge. Ask participants to complete the chart or use their own paper to list facts, concepts, principles, and the like for their discipline *in general (rather than for a specific unit)*.

- Distribute "Matching Content to Core." Ask participants to decide on content for a specific unit. Encourage them to work on this same unit throughout the sessions in this chapter. Point out that while knowledge and skills are certainly important to learning about a discipline, it is the concepts, principles, and often attitudes that carry the most power in sustaining student interest. Remind them that the driving questions of the Core Curriculum Parallel should form the basis of a Core Curriculum unit.

Closure/Looking Forward

If you have time, go on to Workshop #5. Otherwise, end the session by asking participants to critique each others' work, evaluating the degree to which their unit content matches the intents and purposes of the Core Curriculum and/or provides opportunities to address the driving questions of the Core Curriculum.

CONTENT

Definition

Content is what we want students to know, understand, and do as a result of teaching and learning. These ideas are often written as objectives, grade-level expectations, or as broad K–12 standards statements.

Characteristics

Exemplary content and standards incorporate concepts, enduring understandings, and the processes and skills used within a discipline. Additionally, they provide clarity, power, and authenticity for teachers and students.

Category and Definition	*Examples*	*My Discipline or Unit Specific Examples*
FACT A specific detail; verifiable information	• The capital of New York is Albany. • 5 + 7 = 12 • George Washington was the first president of the United States. • The first letter of a new sentence is always capitalized.	
CONCEPT A general idea or understanding; a generalized idea of a thing or a class of things; a category or classification	• Biome • Government • Landscape • Fiction • Integer	

Category and Definition	Examples	My Discipline or Unit Specific Examples
PRINCIPLE A fundamental truth, law, rule, or doctrine that explains the relationship between two or more concepts	• Balance is an important factor in predicting the longevity of a biome. • Forms of government allow for varying amounts of individual freedom. • An artist's use of light changes the rendering of a landscape. • Conflicts arise between protagonists and antagonists. • Two positive numbers can be added in either order. • (1) Not all conflicts can be ended peacefully. (2) Conflicts are caused by differing perspectives. • Adaptation is essential to survival. • Capitals were located near the center of a state and near bodies of water to make it easier to travel. • People must work together to develop laws and policies that they can support and implement. • A balanced diet helps us stay healthy.	
SKILL Proficiency, an ability or a technique; a strategy, a method, or a tool	• Learning how to calculate statistics • Gridding a plot of ground and making systematic observations • Analyzing the plot of a story • Conducting a social action campaign • Comparing and contrasting • Calculating statistics	
ATTITUDES (also known as Dispositions) Beliefs, dispositions, appreciations, and values	• An appreciation of the limits of the environment • A belief in the critical importance of individual democratic rights • An appreciation of the use of light in Impressionist landscapes • A positive attitude toward reading • Intrinsic motivation for learning about real-world data	
PROBLEM SOLVING The ability to transfer and apply acquired knowledge to address a goal	• Identifying the percentage of open land left in a community or state • Developing a strategy to increase parent participation in PTA meetings • Creating a meaningful format for displaying a data set • Creating an original fiction anthology	

Adapted from *The Parallel Curriculum* (Tomlinson, et al., 2008) Figure 3.3.

MATCHING CONTENT TO CORE

Answers to the following questions (adapted from the driving questions of the Core Curriculum) will help you ensure that your content is in sync with the intent and purposes of the Core Curriculum Parallel.

- What does the information in this unit mean to students, as well as to scholars and practitioners of the discipline?
- Why does this information matter?
- How is the information organized to help *students,* as well as scholars and practitioners, use it better?
- How and why do the ideas in this unit make sense?
- What are these ideas and skills for?
- How do these ideas and skills work?
- How can *students,* as well as scholars and practitioners, use these ideas and skills?

WORKSHOP #5

Assessment Component of a Core Curriculum Unit

Session Overview

In this workshop, participants will examine what the assessment component should look like in a Core Curriculum unit. They will also work to design or revise their own unit assessments to match the intent and purposes of this parallel.

Masters

- Assessment
- Sample Assessments for the Core Curriculum
- A Rubric for Measuring Growth in Concept Attainment
- A Rubric for Measuring the Acquisition of Principles and Rules
- Matching Assessment to Core

Session Details

Introduction

- Tell participants that once they are clear on the concepts, principles, skills, and so on for their lessons (or units), they need to craft assessment tools to: (1) identify students' prior knowledge, understanding, and skill in the content to be studied, and (2) measure growth with regard to the major facts, concepts, principles, skills, and dispositions within the topic.
- Explain that checking to see where each child is in the learning process helps guide teachers when writing and executing curriculum and also helps students track their own development and growth. Therefore, we will focus now on the next key component of curriculum: ongoing assessment, including preassessment.
- Distribute "Assessment" and discuss the definitions, characteristics, and possible formats of assessments.

Teaching and Learning Activities

- Teachers assess students in a myriad of ways. Some assessment methods might be informal while others are more formal. Concept maps or expository essays with supporting evidence are more formal ways; engaging in conversations and observations are more informal formats.

Say: "To be effective, assessments must first be aligned to the learning goals. Second, they should be honest and accurate measures of students' learning over time. Third, they must provide some kind of performance or product with which to evaluate student learning. Assessments are used before, during, and after instruction. High-quality assessments inform instruction. Assessments in the Parallel Curriculum Model (PCM) focus on student growth related to core concepts, principles, and skills."

- Share one or more of the examples on "Sample Assessments for the Core Curriculum." Work with participants to judge/discuss the extent to which the example preassessments include a focus on concepts or principles, and make suggestions for how to ensure or highlight this focus. Ask participants if they think the assessments provide a high enough ceiling and low enough baseline to identify the full range of current learning.
- Remind participants that assessments they include in their unit should lead them to information about the extent to which students have attained the content of the unit and can answer the driving questions of the Core Curriculum Parallel. Because the Core Parallel Curriculum emphasizes concept attainment, assessments and accompanying rubrics must measure student growth in concept, principle, and disposition attainment as well as acquisition of knowledge and skill. Care should be taken to ensure that rubrics do not emphasize the quantity or mechanics of a product (e.g., neatness, proper spelling, and number of bibliographic entries) over the quality of knowledge, understanding, and skill.
- Distribute "A Rubric for Measuring Growth in Concept Attainment" and "A Rubric for Measuring the Acquisition of Principles and Rules." In small groups, have participants (1) discuss ways these rubrics meet this challenge and (2) consider the extent to which their own rubrics ensure a focus on concepts and principles.
- End the session by distributing "Matching Assessment to Core." Suggest to participants that they use their classroom textbooks and other textbooks and resources to gather material to create their own assessments, both formative and summative, for their targeted unit (e.g., quizzes, concept maps, portfolios, discussion questions). They also will need to design rubrics that meet the goals of the unit and the intent and purposes of the Core Curriculum Parallel for some or all of these assessments.

Note to Facilitator

You may wish to focus separate sessions on preassessment, on other types of formative assessments—such as journal prompts, quizzes, homework assignments—and on summative assessments such as tests, projects, and performance assessments.

Closure/Looking Forward

Ask participants to critique each others' work, evaluating the degree to which their assessments match the intents and purposes of the Core Curriculum and/or provide opportunities to address the driving questions of the Core Curriculum.

ASSESSMENT

Definition

Assessments are varied tools, techniques, and criteria teachers use to determine the extent or nature of student proficiency with a lesson's or unit's content standards in order to modify instructional plans and support student success.

Characteristics

Assessments are used before, during, and after instruction to inform instruction and measure student learning. Well-designed assessments are diagnostic, are aligned with the learning goals, and provide a high ceiling, as well as a low baseline, to ensure that all students' learning can be measured.

Some Possible Assessment Formats

Oral Questions	Conversations	Recitations
Tests	Essays	Behaviors
Observations	Portfolios	Performances
Think-Alouds	Rubrics	Lab Reports
Running Records	Concept Maps	Auditions
Conferences	Work Products	Assignments

Adapted from *The Parallel Curriculum* (Tomlinson, et al., 2008) Figure 3.2.

SAMPLE ASSESSMENTS FOR THE CORE CURRICULUM

Example 1: Short Story Assessment

1. On a separate sheet of paper, create a web using the following words and phrases in a way that you think makes sense.

Third Person	Plot	Central Conflict
When	Character	Introduction
First Person	Rising Action	Time
Where	Theme	Place
Point of View	Protagonist	Elements
Central Message	Antagonist	Climax
Character	Resolution	Falling Action
Setting		

2. Write a paragraph that explains your web. You may use the back of the paper you used to create the web.

Example 2: Fractions Assessment

Directions: You have 15 minutes to complete these four questions.

1. What is a fraction? Write a few complete sentences to explain.

2. Which is bigger, one-half or one-sixth? Use words, pictures, or both to show how you know which one is bigger.

3. Show two-sixths by shading this pie. →

4. Explain in writing or with pictures why five-fifths is the same as a whole.

5. In what ways might people use fractions in everyday life?

Example 3: Vocabulary Assessment

The following words are taken from the first half of the novel we are about to read. Please highlight those words that you know how to use in a sentence and can define.

Abate	Momentum	Reluctant
Ostentatious	Elaborate	Penchant
Simultaneous	Happenstance	Incorrigible
Subtle	Honorary	Jovial
Concomitant	Protagonist	Probe

Use the words you highlighted in a brief story that shows you know the meaning of each word *and* can use each word correctly in a grammatical sense. Underline the vocabulary words that you use in your story so that I can readily find each one when I read. Please write your story on a separate sheet of paper.

Example 4: Beginning, Middle, and End Preassessment

We will be learning about the beginning, middle, and end of a story.

Think about your whole day. What part of the day does this picture show: *beginning, middle,* or *end*? Write the word you think it shows on the line _____.

We will read a story in class. Use the boxes below and draw a picture or write words or sentences to show the beginning, middle, and end of the story.

Beginning	Middle	End

Example 5: American Independence Preassessment

You will not be graded on this assessment. It is for me to use to plan our upcoming unit based on what you already know or do not know. You may skip questions you do not have answers for, but you can also guess at an answer.

1. Number the following events in the order each happened by writing *1* for the first event, *2* for the second event, and so on in the space provided.

   _____ The Constitution was ratified (approved).

   _____ The war for American independence (American Revolution) ends.

   _____ The Declaration of Independence is written.

   _____ The Boston Tea Party takes place.

   _____ George Washington presents his farewell address.

2. Explain what "all men are created equal" meant to most Americans leaders at the time the Declaration of Independence was written.

3. What does the word *revolution* mean?

4. How is the word *revolution* associated with early America and the colonists?

5. Tell briefly why each of the following persons, terms, or events is important. Use a separate sheet of paper for this.

a. Benjamin Franklin	e. George Washington	i. Articles of Confederation
b. Boston Massacre	f. Boston Tea Party	j. Declaration of Independence
c. Thomas Paine	g. Sons of Liberty	k. Loyalists
d. King George	h. Tories	1. Lexington and Concord

6. Using the blank map your teacher provides, write in each of the colonies that you know.

A RUBRIC FOR MEASURING GROWTH IN CONCEPT ATTAINMENT

	Beginning	Developing	Competent	Proficient	Expert
Level of Understanding	The learner communicates the term associated with the abstract concept.	The learner paraphrases the definition of the concept.	The learner provides example and nonexamples of the concept.	The learner provides key attributes that distinguish the concept category.	The learner links the concept with other related concepts.
Example	Migration	"Migration is movement of living things for a real reason or purpose."	Examples: Butterflies, Whales, Salmon Nonexamples: When a subdivision is built, Fires, Accidents	Beneficial Change Large groups Movement Purposeful Causes Effects Universal	"People and animals migrate to improve their chances to meet their needs."

A RUBRIC FOR MEASURING THE ACQUISITION OF PRINCPLES AND RULES

	Beginning	Developing	Competent	Proficient	Expert
Level of Understanding	The learner defines and provides examples of the key concepts within a rule or principle.	The learner identifies a relationship between two or more concepts.	The learner explains the relationship as conditional, if/then, cause/effect, part/whole.	The learner provides novel examples of the principle or rule within a discipline or field of study.	The learner provides novel examples of the principle across disciplines or fields of study.
Example	Butterflies Whales Salmon	"Animals move around to get what they need."	"Animal migration is all about reasons and results."	"We studied whale migration in class but migration happens a lot in biology, for example, with butterflies and even people."	"Migration in animals is like the Westward Movement in history."

Adapted from *The Parallel Curriculum* (Tomlinson, et al., 2002) Figures 4.5 and 4.6.

MATCHING ASSESSMENT TO CORE

Study your assessments one at a time. Your answers to the following questions (modified from the driving questions of the Core Curriculum) will help you ensure that your assessments are in sync with the intent and purposes of the Core Curriculum Parallel.

To what degree does your assessment help students explain:

- The *meaning* of unit information? (i.e., does it focus solely on facts and skills or does it also measure students' understanding of concepts and principles?)
- Why the unit information matters?
- How to use the information?
- How and why the ideas in this unit make sense?
- What these ideas and skills are for?
- How these ideas and skills work?

WORKSHOP #6

Introductory Activities Component of a Core Curriculum Unit

Session Overview

In this workshop, participants will examine what introductory activities might look like in a Core Curriculum unit. They also will work to design or revise their own unit introductory activities to match the intent and purposes of this parallel.

Masters

- Introductory Activities
- Sample Introductory Activities
- Matching Introduction to Core

Session Details

Introduction

- Begin by asking participants to discuss the purpose of introductory activities and to share successful examples from their own classrooms.
- After the discussion, distribute "Introductory Activities."

Say: "Introductory activities are often overlooked or underused. The decision to hasten or eliminate these experiences can short-circuit student learning. The quality and comprehensiveness of introductory activities often predicts the degree to which all students can develop rich schemes of thought, analogies, and deep understanding of content. The shared conversations, examples, experiences, and questions posed during introductory activities create a bond among the family of learners. They also provide a shared anchor that the teacher can reference during the remainder of the study to foster acquisition of content."

Teaching and Learning Activities

- Distribute "Sample Introductory Activities." Make the point that introductory activities in a Core Curriculum unit should help students focus on the concepts and principles of a given unit. Ask teachers to identify ways in which the sample introductory activities do—or don't—accomplish this goal.
- Distribute "Matching Introduction to Core." In grade- and/or subject-alike groups, have participants work on creating introductory activities for their unit that are clearly linked to the intents and purposes of the Core Curriculum Parallel.

Closure/Looking Forward

Ask participants to critique each others' work, evaluating the degree to which their introductory activities match the intents and purposes of the Core Curriculum and/or provide opportunities to address the driving questions of the Core Curriculum.

INTRODUCTORY ACTIVITIES

Definition

An introduction sets the stage for a unit. Components may include (1) a focusing question, (2) an assessment to determine students' prior knowledge, interests, and learning preferences, (3) a teaser or "hook" to motivate students, (4) information about the real world relevance of the goals and unit expectations, (5) information about expectations for students, and (6) consideration of students' interests in or experiences that connect with the unit topic.

Characteristics

A high-quality introduction likely will include many of these elements, as well as an advance organizer that provides students with information that they can use to help assess their acquisition of the unit's learning goals.

Concept Maps or Webs	Use lines, arrows, and oval shapes to build a map that will depict the relationships among facts, concepts, principles, and representative topics, and the discipline.
Focusing or Guiding Questions	Explore the nature of the concepts, relationships among the concepts, principles, facts, and skills central to the Core study.
Advance Organizers	Develop and share advance organizers that support development of concepts and principles.
Introduction	Use an introduction to explain how the topic students are studying is representative of the discipline at large.
Learning Experiences	Show students what experts at the frontier of the discipline investigate.

Adapted from *The Parallel Curriculum* (Tomlinson, et al., 2008) Figure 3.2.

Possible Formats

SAMPLE INTRODUCTORY ACTIVITIES

Example 1

As an introduction to a government unit, a teacher posts the following guiding questions for the unit. He begins by asking students to think, pair, and share answers to one of more of the questions.

- Why do we have laws?
- How are laws formed?
- How does the system of checks and balances affect how laws are made and passed?
- How do laws affect our lives?

Example 2

As an introduction to a unit on the structure of plants, an elementary teacher displays and discusses with students the following diagram:

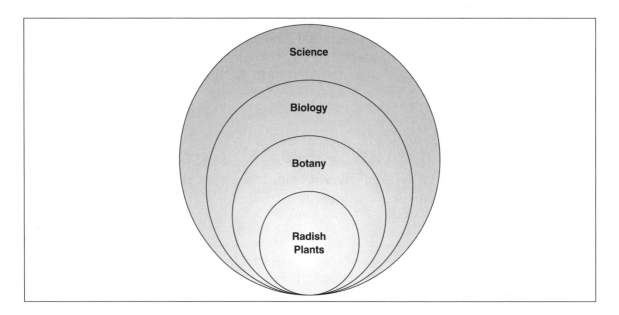

Example 3

As an introduction to a literature unit, a teacher posts the following graphic organizer on the board:

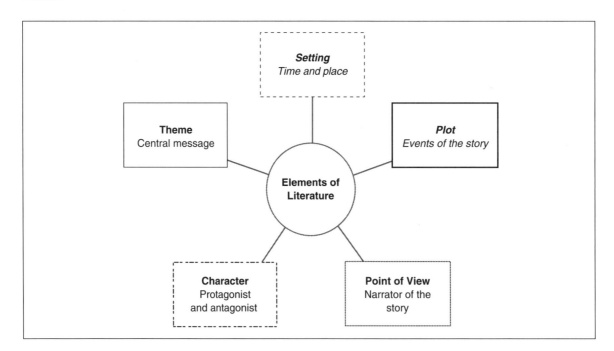

Example 4

As an introduction to a unit on the Civil War, a teacher distributes photographs from the mid-1800s and asks students to identify both familiar and unfamiliar elements.

Example 5

As an introduction to a unit on fractions, a teacher asks students to share an example of a time when they had to share food with friends or family.

Example 6

As an introduction to the study of physics, a teacher shares a list of the eleven greatest unanswered questions of physics from an article by Eric Haseltine (2002) in the online magazine *Discover: Science, Technology and the Future.*

MATCHING INTRODUCTION TO CORE

Your answers to the following questions (modified from the driving questions of the Core Curriculum) will help you ensure that your introductory activities are in sync with the intent and purposes of the Core Curriculum Parallel

To what degree do your introductory activities:

- Focus on the *meaning* of unit information?
- Inform students about how and why they will want to use unit information?
- Show students the overall structure and goals of the unit?
- Generate excitement and enthusiasm?
- Provide opportunities for students to share prior, related student knowledge?

Consider: To what degree should or could your introductory activities be tailored for varied student interests and/or learning preferences?

WORKSHOP #7

Teaching Strategies Component of a Core Curriculum Unit

Session Overview

In this workshop, participants will examine and make decisions about teaching strategies appropriate for a Core Curriculum unit. They also will work to design, revise, and/or expand their own teaching strategies to match the intent and purposes of this parallel.

Masters

- Teaching Strategies
- Sample Teaching Strategies

(Continued)

(Continued)

- Bingo Cards
- Matching Strategies to Core

Session Details

Introduction

To begin this lesson, say: "As a teacher, you employ methods or strategies to instruct students or connect them with the content you want to teach. The best teaching methods or strategies support the learning goals within a unit of study and help the teacher work more as a facilitator, trainer, and/or coach, rather than a mere dispenser of knowledge. There is a multitude of teaching strategies, yet many of us tend to use the same ones over and over again. When you stand in the front of the room and deliver content, you are using what teaching method or strategy? (Answer: lecture.) When you orchestrate students in a way that involves them as participants and observers in a simulation in which they assume real-world situations, what teaching method have you used?" (Answer: role playing.)

Distribute and read "Teaching Strategies." Ask participants to share their favorite teaching strategies. Ask them to identify ways in which these strategies benefit both the teacher and the student.

Teaching and Learning Activities

Conduct one (or a combination) of the following activities as appropriate to your audience. The labels *Novice, Intermediate,* and *Advanced* refer to the degree to which teachers are already familiar with a wide variety of teaching strategies.

Novice Activities

1. Matching Game

- Conduct an activity in which participants work in pairs, trios, or small groups to match teaching methods with their definitions. To do this, copy the "Sample Teaching Strategies" sheet onto heavy bond paper. Then use a cutting board to cut **each** teaching method from its definitions. At the end of this preparation, you will have a complete set in an envelope with twenty-one teaching methods and twenty-one definitions—forty-two pieces in all inside each envelope. You will need to prepare several sets so that each pair, trio, or small group has its own envelope of forty-two pieces.
- Allow participants to spend time reading and inferring which teaching method corresponds to each definition. Walk around the room to gauge how much time is needed to complete this activity. When all are finished, have each pair or small group share its matches. Have other participants agree or disagree with matches. If disagreement ensues, ask participants to share how they arrived at a match. As facilitator, settle any stalemates.
- Distribute a copy of "Sample Teaching Strategies" to each participant for future reference.

2. Bingo Game

- To prepare for the game, do the following.
  - Three versions of Bingo cards are coded with a symbol on either side of the title (◨●◻) so facilitators know the difference.
  - Find covers for the spaces, such as paper circles, tiddly-wink chips, pennies, or beans.
  - Take out the "Sample Teaching Strategies" handout that includes all twenty-one strategies. Using a cutting board, cut out strips for each definition only and put these twenty-one strips in a hat or bucket. During the game, you will pull strips at random and read them.

- To play the game, randomly distribute a BINGO board to each participant or pair of participants. When distributing cards, be sure that those sitting next to each other have different cards.
- Explain how the game will be played:
  - ○ Each player gets a Bingo card and a handful of covers for spaces.
  - ○ Players listen as each teaching method definition is read.
  - ○ If a teaching method described is listed on a participant's Bingo card, that person covers that space.
  - ○ The winner is the player who has four spaces covered: all corners or all in a row horizontally or vertically.
  - ○ Once a winner is identified, review the definitions for each space covered to verify that the definition matches the teaching method.
- Distribute a copy of "Sample Teaching Strategies" to each participant for future reference.

3. Scenario Match

- Distribute a copy of "Sample Teaching Strategies" to each participant for reference. One at a time, read aloud or project each classroom situation in the table that follows. Then, have participants use the handout to determine which specific teaching method is applicable to each situation.

Classroom Situation	Answer
In a third grade class, Mrs. Tuchman shows various slides and laminated pictures of personification and asks students what they notice that is the same about the group of visuals. She then shows nonexamples and asks what is missing in these pictures that are different than the first set.	Concept Attainment
In a middle school science class, Mrs. House conducts a PowerPoint presentation and provides an explanation of the slides to build students' knowledge base of atomic theory. She pauses at various intervals to allow students to reflect and clarify.	Lecture
To introduce a unit on feudalism (social structure), Mrs. Glass has her students line up outside the classroom door. She ushers students in one at a time and guides each to one of three places in the classroom: (1) a table beautifully decorated with candelabra, tablecloth, and fabric-backed chairs covered with luscious, mouthwatering food and drink; (2) a smaller table with objects related to medieval churches and utilitarian foods that would be eaten during medieval times; (3) a spot on the floor for eating stale bread.	Simulation

Intermediate Activity

- Distribute a copy of "Sample Teaching Strategies" to each participant for reference. Divide up the teaching strategies listed and ask participants to write or describe a plausible scenario from their own classroom in which they use that strategy. (You may use the scenarios in the Scenario Match activity as exemplars for this activity.) They should then take turns asking other group members to identify the teaching strategy(s) used. For extra challenge, ask participants to devise a few scenarios that combine teaching strategies in a logical way.

Advanced Activity

- Brainstorm as comprehensive a list of strategies as possible.

Say: "The strategies we use in the classroom may be seen as falling along a continuum that ranges from indirect to direct."

(Continued)

(Continued)

- Make large cards of each teaching method. To do this, copy on heavy bond paper and cut from the "Sample Teaching Methods" sheet used earlier. Have each participant choose one card so each is then holding the name of a teaching method. Clear a space for participants to stand along an imaginary line. Designate one end of the line as "direct" and the other end "indirect." Instruct participants to circulate around the room and read each other's cards. Then, ask them to stand on the appropriate spot on the line that represents to what degree the teaching method they are holding is direct or indirect. (Depending on the size of your group, you may wish to make a set of 5×7 index cards for every four or five participants and ask them to arrange the cards on a table or wall rather than arranging themselves.)
- After all participants have arranged themselves from least to most directive, distribute "Sample Teaching Strategies," which is arranged along this continuum with direct teaching activities at the beginning of the chart and less directed activities at the end. Thus, strategies become more indirect as the figure continues. Discuss any discrepancies or disagreements.
- Ask teachers how they make decisions about whether to use a direct or indirect teaching strategy in a particular lesson. Ask them to use specific examples from their own classrooms. (The decision to use a direct or indirect method likely will hinge on the amount of available instructional time, access to resources at students' independent reading levels, students' proficiency with various analytic thinking skills, and students' prior knowledge in the content area.)

Teaching and Learning Activities Continued

- Ask participants to discuss the following in small groups. (If possible, regroup participants so that there is a mixture of expertise levels in each small group.)
  - Which strategies on the list are particularly comfortable ones for you and/or your students? Why do you think this is the case?
  - Which strategies on the list are unfamiliar to you? Ask your colleagues for help in thinking of ways to incorporate those strategies into your teaching.
  - Which strategies would particularly appeal to struggling learners? Advanced learners? Other special needs students? Introverts? Extroverts?
- Pose the following question to the whole group: Which of the teaching strategies on our list would be an especially good fit for a Core Curriculum unit? Why do you say so? (Encourage them to focus on ways in which the various strategies help teachers and learners focus on concepts and principles.)
- Distribute "Matching Strategies to Core." Have participants work with their own unit to incorporate opportunities for using a variety of teaching strategies. Suggest that participants try to incorporate at least one strategy that is new to them or their students. Remind teachers that it is important to vary teaching strategies throughout a given unit, but that strategies used in a Core Curriculum unit should allow teachers and students to focus on the key concepts and principles of the unit.

Closure/Looking Forward

Ask participants to critique each others' work, evaluating the degree to which their strategies match the intents and purposes of the Core Curriculum and/or provide opportunities to address the driving questions of the Core Curriculum.

TEACHING STRATEGIES

Definition

Teaching strategies are methods teachers use to support student learning. These techniques help teachers introduce, explain, demonstrate, model, coach, guide, transfer, or assess learning.

Characteristics

Beneficial teaching methods are closely aligned to research, learning goals, and learner characteristics. They are varied, promote student involvement, and provide support and feedback.

Adapted from *The Parallel Curriculum* (Tomlinson, et al., 2008) Figure 3.2.

SAMPLE TEACHING STRATEGIES

Teaching Method	Definition
Lecture	Carefully sequenced, often illustrated, oral presentation of content that is delivered to small and large groups of students; oral presentation should be interspersed with opportunities for reflection, clarification, and sense making.
Drill and Recitation	Strategy used to help students memorize and recall information with accuracy and speed.
Direct Instruction	Teacher's systematic explanation of a new concept or skill followed by guided practice under a teacher's guidance.
Strategy-Based Instruction	Used to teach a cognitive strategy or procedure; teacher explains and helps students acquire the strategy, models the strategy, and provides guided practice and feedback to students as they internalize the strategy.
Assisted Instruction in the Content Areas	Range of methods used to support or scaffold students' reading of nonfiction material in various content fields.
Graphic Organizer	Visual diagrams used to help students understand content and thinking strategies.
Coaching	Criterion-referenced observations made about student performance; immediate, specific feedback is provided to improve student performance.
Concept Attainment	Used to help students understand the essential attributes of a category or concept; teacher leads students through a controlled discussion as students compare and contrast characteristics of examples and nonexamples of the category or concept.

(Continued)

(Continued)

Teaching Method	Definition
Synectics	Teachers and students share or develop metaphors, similes, and/or analogies that build a bridge between students' prior knowledge or experience and new learning.
Demonstration/ Modeling	Teacher's actions and behaviors serve as an example for students who then replicate the actions and behaviors in other contexts.
Socratic Questioning	A carefully constructed sequence of questions posed to help students improve their logical reasoning and critical thinking about their position on an issue.
Visualization	Students are encouraged to pretend and imagine; students do not speak; they can be asked to see themselves performing a skill or participating in an event.
Role Playing	Students are participants or observers in a simulation of a real-world situation.
Cooperative Learning	Small group interaction used to forward new learning and accomplish academic and social tasks.
Jurisprudence	Students collaborate to develop cases and persuasive arguments on all sides of an issue, controversy, or decision.
Simulation	Students assume roles of people engaged in complex, real-life situations.
Inquiry-Based Instruction	Students explore a task, problem, or intriguing situation across small changes in the data set and generate insights about the problem and/or solutions.
Problem Solving and Problem-Based Learning	Students investigate and collaboratively solve an ill-structured, novel, and complex problem with teacher guidance and coaching.
Shadowing Experiences	A student, or a small group of students, receives short-term exposure to practitioners in selected fields or disciplines; may involve several hours or days.
Mentorship	A student spends some time collaborating with an expert in the field to learn the content, methodology, and day-to-day activities of the practicing professional.
Independent Study	Individuals or small groups are encouraged to explore self-selected areas of study.

Adapted from *The Parallel Curriculum* (Tomlinson, et al., 2002) Figure 3.7.

BINGO CARDS

◎ BINGO ◎

Lecture	Mentorship	Simulation	Strategy-Based Instruction
Graphic Organizer	Drill	Independent Study	Synectics
Socratic Questioning	Coaching	Direct Instruction	Inquiry-Based Instruction
Jurisprudence	Visualization	Concept Attainment	Role Playing

● BINGO ●

Problem Solving	Shadowing Experiences	Graphic Organizer	Mentorship
Assisted Instruction	Strategy-Based Instruction	Drill	Visualization
Demonstration	Coaching	Direct Instruction	Simulation
Cooperative Learning	Independent Study	Jurisprudence	Socratic Questioning

❑ BINGO ❑

Mentorship	Graphic Organizer	Inquiry-Based Instruction	Independent Study
Socratic Questioning	Role Playing	Concept Attainment	Lecture
Drill	Jurisprudence	Assisted Instruction	Demonstration
Problem Solving	Simulation	Shadowing Experiences	Coaching

MATCHING STRATEGIES TO CORE

Your answers to the following questions (modified from the driving questions of the Core Curriculum) will help you ensure that the teaching strategies you incorporate into your unit are in sync with the intent and purposes of the Core Curriculum Parallel.

To what degree do your teaching strategies:

- Encourage you and your students to focus on the *meaning* of unit information?
- Inform students about how and why they will want to use unit ideas and skills?
- Show students how the ideas and skills in the unit fit into the ideas and skills of the discipline as a whole?
- Allow you to respond to variation in student preferences for acquiring unit information?

WORKSHOP #8

Learning Activities Component of a Core Curriculum Unit

Session Overview

In this workshop, participants will consider what learning activities might be appropriate for a Core Curriculum unit. They also will work to design, revise, and/or expand their own unit learning activities to match the intent and purposes of this parallel.

Masters

- Learning Activities
- Learning Activity Suggestions for the Core Curriculum Parallel
- Matching Activities to Core

Session Details

Introduction

Say: "*Teaching strategies* allow you to instruct students or connect them with the content. *Learning activities* are tasks for students that we design to help them develop the knowledge, understanding, and skills specified in the content goals. Learning activities should call on students to engage thoughtfully with unit information.

Think about an activity you have conducted in class for a specific unit. What learning activities did you employ? In what ways did the activities make it possible for students to explore the content area? In what ways did the activities emphasize concepts, principles, and generalizations? What happens when learning activities are not closely tied to unit goals?"

Teaching and Learning Activities

- Show and/or distribute "Learning Activities." Introduce the four types of thinking that learning activities typically address: analytical, critical, executive, and creative. Ask participants to scan the list of skills for each type of thinking and take turns sharing one or two examples of learning activities that introduce or foster a particular type of thinking. Try to solicit examples from each of the four types of thinking.
- Hold a discussion around this question: In your opinion, what kinds of learning activities best support the goals of the Core Curriculum Parallel? Why do you say so?
- Display or distribute "Learning Activity Suggestions for the Core Curriculum Parallel" and discuss ways in which participants' thoughts matched or did not match these examples.
- Have participants use the suggestions on this handout to work with their targeted unit to remodel or create learning activities that support the intent and purposes of the Core Curriculum Parallel. Be sure to constantly check that the activities they design have a clear and visible connection to unit concepts and principles. Encourage participants to balance opportunities for the four types of thinking in their unit activities.

Closure/Looking Forward

End the session by distributing "Matching Activities to Core." Ask participants to use this handout to critique each others' work, evaluating the degree to which their activities match the intents and purposes of the Core Curriculum and/or provide opportunities to address the driving questions of the Core Curriculum.

LEARNING ACTIVITIES

Definition

A unit's learning activities are those cognitive experiences that help students perceive, process, rehearse, store, and transfer knowledge, understanding, and skill.

Characteristics

Effective learning activities are aligned with the learning goals and efficiently foster cognitive engagement via a variety of thinking skills (see below).

Thinking Skill	Definition
Analytical-Thinking Skills	**Various cognitive processes that deepen understanding of knowledge and skills**
Identifying characteristics	The ability to identify distinct, specific, and relevant details that characterize an object, an event, or a phenomenon
Recognizing attributes	The facility to discern and label general or common features of a set of objects
Making observations	The capability to perceive and select attributes of an object or experience
Discriminating between same and different	The ability to make fine discriminations among objects, ideas, or events
Comparing and contrasting	The facility to see similarities and differences same among objects, events, and people
Categorizing	The ability to group objects or events according to some preconceived classification scheme
Classifying	The capability to extract relevant attributes of a group of objects, people, or phenomena that can be used to sort or organize the same
Ranking, prioritizing, and sequencing	The facility to place objects, events, or phenomena in hierarchical order according to some quantifiable value
Seeing relationships	The ability to see a connection or interaction between two or more objects or phenomena
Finding patterns	The ability to perceive and extract a repeating scheme in objects or phenomena
Determining cause and effect	The ability to see and extract the most powerful reasons or results for a given event or action
Predicting	The ability to see patterns, compare and contrast, identify relationships, determine cause and effect, and anticipate likely events in the future
Making analogies	The ability to identify a relationship between two familiar items or events and similar items and events in order to problem¬solve or initiate creative productivity
Critical-Thinking Skills	**Various thinking skills that are used to analyze and evaluate data and evidence in order to develop, judge the effectiveness of, or respond to an argument or position**
Inductive thinking	The ability to draw an inferential conclusion based on repeated observations that yield consistent but incomplete data
Deductive thinking	The ability to draw a logical conclusion from premises
Determining benefits and drawbacks	The ability to weight the advantages and disadvantages of a given idea or action
Determining reality and fantasy	The ability to distinguish between that which is fanciful and that which is true or actual
Identifying value statements	The ability to recognize statements that reflect appraisals of worth that cannot be supported through objective means
Identifying points of view	The ability to recognize that individuals and groups may have values and beliefs that influence their perspective on issues
Determining bias	The ability to ascertain information that is value laden
Identifying fact and opinion	The ability to distinguish between statements that can be proven and statements that reflect personal beliefs or judgments
Judging essential and incidental evidence	The ability to assess information and categorize it into useful and less useful categories
Identifying missing information	The ability to determine essential information that is not given or provided

Thinking Skill	Definition
Judging the accuracy of information	The ability to determine the precision of evidence that is presented
Judging the credibility of a source	The ability to assess whether the given information is believable, valid, and worthy to be considered
Recognizing assumptions	The ability to distinguish between information that is commonly accepted as true and information that is conjecture
Determining the strength of an argument	The ability to extract the reasons for an argument and evaluate the evidence as worthy
Identifying exaggeration	The ability to extract statements that magnify or overstate what is accepted as fact
Executive Processes	**Various cognitive skills that are involved in organizing, synthesizing, generalizing, or applying knowledge**
Summarizing	The ability to reduce a written or oral narrative to its essential components
Metacognition	The ability to consciously monitor, describe, and reflect upon one's thinking
Setting goals	The ability to set desirable outcomes in any situation
Formulating questions	The ability to develop relevant and precise queries related to any endeavor
Developing hypotheses	The ability to use prior observations to develop a possible explanation for an apparent relationship between two variables
Generalizing	The ability to use repeated, controlled, and accurate observations to develop a rule, principle, or formula that explains a number of situations
Problem solving	The ability to describe a problem, identify an ideal outcome, and to select and test possible strategies and solutions
Decision making	The ability to create and use appropriate criteria to select the best alternative in a given situation
Planning	The ability to develop a detailed and sequenced series of actions to achieve an end
Creative Thinking Skills	**Various cognitive skills that are involved in creative production**
Fluency	The ability to generate numerous ideas or alternatives to solve a problem that requires a novel solution
Flexibility	The ability to generate a wide variety of ideas to solve a problem that requires a novel solution
Originality	The ability to generate novel or unique alternatives to solve a problem that requires a novel solution
Elaboration	The ability to create a large number of details that explain a novel solution to a problem
Imagery	The ability to visualize a situation or object and to manipulate various alternatives for solving a problem without benefit of models, props, or physical objects
Using idea/product modification techniques	The ability to use techniques such as substituting, combining, techniques adapting, modifying, making larger or smaller, putting to new uses, eliminating, reversing, or rearranging parts to make a more useful whole
Listing attributes	The ability to identify appropriate improvements to a process or product by systematically considering modifications to the original product's attributes
Brainstorming	The ability to work with others to withhold judgment while identifying varied, innovative, and numerous alternatives for solving a problem
Creative problem solving	The ability to identify, research, and plan to solve a problem that requires a novel, systematic solution

Adapted from *The Parallel Curriculum* (Tomlinson, et al., 2008) Figure 3.2.

LEARNING ACTIVITY SUGGESTIONS
FOR THE CORE CURRICULUM PARALLEL

- Have students analyze and talk about examples, information, and data in small groups using a cooperative learning or guided discussion format.
- Have students use raw data, examples, events, and observations to detect patterns and draw conclusions.
- Ask students to suggest and test principles.
- Have students identify patterns and categories.
- Ask students to work as firsthand inquirers and analysts in the discipline.
- Have students focus on analytic skills, problem-solving skills, and skills of the discipline.
- Include experiments, simulations, and problem-solving activities.
- Have students note characteristics and attributes, and search for patterns, sequences, and relationships.

Adapted from *The Parallel Curriculum* (Tomlinson, et al., 2008) Figure 4.2.

MATCHING ACTIVITIES TO CORE

Your answers to the following questions (modified from the driving questions of the Core Curriculum) will help you ensure that the learning activities you incorporate into your unit are in sync with the intent and purposes of the Core Curriculum Parallel.

To what degree do your learning activities help all students:

- Focus on the *meaning* of unit information?
- Practice unit ideas and skills?
- Think analytically, creatively, executively, and critically?
- Identify and demonstrate how the ideas and skills in the unit fit into the ideas and skills of the discipline as a whole?

WORKSHOP #9

Grouping Practices Component of a Core Curriculum Unit

Session Overview

In this workshop, participants will determine ways to group students for learning so that the grouping choices support the intent and purposes of this parallel.

Masters

- Grouping Practices
- Grouping Practices Suggestions for the Core Curriculum Parallel
- Matching Grouping Practices to Core

Session Details

Introduction

Begin this session by saying:	"Grouping strategies enable teachers to arrange students in configurations most likely to enhance the acquisition of content, skills, principles, and so on. Decisions about grouping should be based on content goals and the needs of the students involved, and they should include both the directions and support necessary to ensure that students know how to work successfully in the particular grouping configuration." "Opportunities for students to work in pairs or small groups facilitate the analytic and reflective dialogue among learners that fosters concept attainment, the development of principles and generalizations, and the acquisition of methodological, cognitive, and inquiry skills."

Distribute and discuss "Grouping Practices." Invite teachers to share their personal classroom experiences with using these and other grouping formats.

Ask:	"Which grouping formats are your favorites as a teacher? What were your favorites when you were a student? Are they the same in both cases? Why or why not?"

Teaching and Learning Activities

- Facilitate discussion by using the following questions.
  - There are multiple ways to group students for any particular learning experience. In your opinion, what factors should teachers consider when deciding on a particular type of grouping for a particular lesson? (Learning goals, student characteristics, support needed to facilitate group, and so forth should be factors they consider.)
  - What are potential trouble spots in the various types of groupings?
  - How can we deal with these obstacles?
  - Why is it important that groupings change over time?
- Distribute or display "Grouping Practices Suggestions for the Core Curriculum Parallel." Ask participants to use these suggestions to help them decide when and how to group students for the unit activities they have planned so far. Encourage them to design additional unit activities that expand their use of varied grouping practices. Remind them that they should be able to explain how their grouping practices support unit goals, respond to student variance, and match the intents and purposes of the Core Curriculum Parallel.

Closure/Looking Forward

End the session by distributing "Matching Grouping Practices to Core." Ask participants to critique each others' work, looking for variety of grouping strategies over time and evaluating the degree to which their grouping choices support the intents and purposes of the Core Curriculum and/or provide opportunities to address the driving questions of the Core Curriculum.

GROUPING PRACTICES

Definition

Grouping strategies refer to varied approaches a teacher can use to arrange students for effective learning in the classroom.

Characteristics

Well-designed grouping strategies are aligned with the learning goals. Effective grouping strategies are varied and change frequently to accommodate students' interests, questions, learning preferences, prior knowledge, or learning rate and zone of proximal development. Group membership changes frequently based on learning goals and assessment of student learning.

Possible Grouping Formats

Whole Group Instruction	A grouping strategy that is used to enhance learning when all students have approximately the same level of prior knowledge and there are no critical differences in learning style preferences, interests, effort, or motivation.
Cooperative Learning Groups	A grouping technique in which learners participate in small teams on similar tasks. The strategy is based on social learning theory, which states that increased learning results when students engage in discussion, think-alouds, and other forms of verbal interaction.
Flexible, Small Groups	A grouping strategy that is used to enhance learning when significant differences exist among students. Flexible, small groups of students (two to ten members) are formed for short periods to address critical differences in students' interests, learning style preferences, questions, motivation, expression style preference, prior knowledge, readiness to learn, and learning rate. Group tasks are different and honor student differences. These groups can be led by a teacher or students. They also can be designed as collaborative teaching and learning activities.
Dyads	A grouping strategy in which students are paired for a variety of purposes: to share thinking, to complete a task, to analyze and reflect on a completed task, or to check each other's work, for instance.
Tutoring	A grouping technique in which the teacher works one-on-one with a student. It is used to address unique facets of a learner's prior knowledge or cognitive, social, and emotional profile.

Adapted from *The Parallel Curriculum* (Tomlinson, et al., 2008) Figure 3.2.

GROUPING PRACTICES SUGGESTIONS FOR THE CORE CURRICULUM PARALLEL

- Work with large groups of students to overview the goals of the unit, to provide directions, and to share information about the discipline and representative topic.
- Work with large or small groups of students to facilitate acquisition of essential knowledge.
- Use pairs and small groups of students to support analysis of examples and information as students develop concepts and principles.
- Briefly conference with individual students to assess the degree to which they can relate examples and raw data to core concepts and principles.
- Observe individual students and provide feedback to support the development of analytic thinking.
- Debrief students in large groups, using concept maps and diagrams, to ensure that the entire class can connect activities, data, and examples to core concepts and principles.

Adapted from *The Parallel Curriculum* (Tomlinson, et al., 2008) Figure 4.2.

MATCHING GROUPING PRACTICES TO CORE

Your answers to the following questions (modified from the driving questions of the Core Curriculum) will help you ensure that the learning activities you incorporate into your unit are in sync with the intent and purposes of the Core Curriculum Parallel.

To what degree do your grouping practices help students:

- Maintain a focus on the *meaning* of unit information?
- Practice unit ideas and skills?
- Improve their ability to think analytically, creatively, executively, and critically?
- See the connection between unit ideas and skills and the ideas and skills of the discipline as a whole?

WORKSHOP #10

Resources Component of a Core Curriculum Unit

Session Overview

In this workshop, participants will develop and/or extend their inventory of student and teacher resources as appropriate for a Core Curriculum unit.

Masters

- Resources
- Resources Suggestions for the Core Curriculum Parallel
- Matching Resources to Core

Session Details

Introduction

- Now that teachers are deep in the process of remodeling lessons to be in alignment with the Core Curriculum Parallel, they most likely have given some thought to the student and teacher resources they will use. Distribute and/or display "Resources."
- Ask participants to discuss their experiences with the various resources listed on this sheet. Which ones are new to them? Which ones do they have trouble locating or tend to overlook?

Teaching and Learning Activities

- Remind participants that the Core Parallel is built on key facts, concepts, principles, and skills essential to the discipline and reflects what experts in the discipline find most important.
- Share "Resources Suggestions for the Core Curriculum Parallel." Instruct participants to critically review this sheet in small groups and discuss ways in which these suggestions would help them align their unit to the intents and purposes of the Core Curriculum. Each group should appoint a recorder to jot down five salient points from their discussion. Then, lead a whole group discussion using these points as a springboard for additional ways to use resources.

(Continued)

(Continued)

- Give teachers the opportunity to reflect on their work thus far and to identify those resources they have already incorporated into their unit design. Ask them to continue adding learning activities to their unit that make use of previously untapped resources or types of resources. Instruct participants to ask themselves this question as they work to identify and use appropriate resources: In what ways do these resources reflect the varied interests, learning preferences, and readiness levels of the students?

Closure/Looking Forward

End the session by distributing "Matching Resources to Core." Ask participants to critique each others' work, evaluating the degree to which their resources match the intents and purposes of the Core Curriculum and/or provide opportunities to address the driving questions of the Core Curriculum.

RESOURCES

Definition

Resources are materials that support learning during the teaching and learning activities. Resources should include print and nonprint sources, as well as human resources.

Characteristics

Exemplary resources are varied in format and link closely to the learning goals, students' reading and comprehension levels, and learning preferences.

Adapted from *The Parallel Curriculum* (Tomlinson, et al., 2008) Figure 3.2.

Sample Resources

NONHUMAN			
Print		*Nonprint*	
Biographies	Nonfiction	Software	Experiments
Poems	Fiction	Artifacts	Situations
Plays	Historical Fiction	Tools	Events
Diaries	Literary Analyses	Inventions	Globes
Magazine Articles	Manuals	Technology	Exhibits
Journals	Maps	Antiques	Costumes
Web Sites	Survey Data	Posters	Designs
College Textbooks	Tables	Paintings	Equipment
Textbooks	Charts	Dioramas	Videotapes
Newspapers	Anthologies	Models	Diagrams
E-mails	Historical Documents	Realia	Art Supplies
		Photographs	Musical Instruments
		Observations	Music

Adapted from *The Parallel Curriculum* (Tomlinson, et al., 2008) Figure 3.9.

HUMAN
Content Area Experts
Older Students
Younger Students
Other Students in the Classroom
Parents
Other Teachers of That Grade
Community Members
Teachers from Other Grade Levels
Other School Personnel
University Personnel
Business Personnel
Service Organization Personnel
Retired Senior Citizens

RESOURCES SUGGESTIONS FOR THE CORE CURRICULUM PARALLEL

- Locate, reproduce, and distribute samples of research studies and investigations in the discipline or field.
- Provide biographies of historical and contemporary inquirers, inventors, and researchers in the field.
- Provide journals, blank charts, tables, and diagrams so that students can record their data, reflect on their learning experiences, and outline a schema that represents their understanding of the relationships between concepts and principles.
- Develop and share a format for developing hypotheses, designing studies, recording data, and formulating conclusions.
- Provide students with concept maps and advance organizers that preview the important concepts and principles explored in the unit.
- Provide graphic organizers to support cognitive and methodological skill acquisition.
- Develop clear directions and expectations for data analysis, observations, field studies, and independent study.
- Identify and locate numerous examples related to the concepts addressed in the unit.
- Provide access to Inspiration software to develop concept maps.

Adapted from *The Parallel Curriculum* (Tomlinson, et al., 2008) Figure 4.2.

MATCHING RESOURCES TO CORE

Your answers to the following questions (modified from the driving questions of the Core Curriculum) will help you ensure that the resources you incorporate into your unit are in sync with the intent and purposes of the Core Curriculum Parallel.

To what degree do your resources help you and your students:

- Understand what the unit information means to students as well as scholars and practitioners of the discipline?
- Organize unit information?
- Identify and practice unit ideas and skills?
- Identify and demonstrate how the ideas and skills in the unit fit into the ideas and skills of the discipline as a whole?

WORKSHOP #11

Products Component of a Core Curriculum Unit

Session Overview

In this workshop, participants will determine product assignments that serve to support the intent and purposes of unit goals and the Core Curriculum Parallel.

Masters

- Products
- Product Suggestions for the Core Curriculum Parallel
- Flying Physics Project
- Matching Products to Core

Session Details

Introduction

Tell participants that they have undoubtedly designed a multitude of product assessments in their day. For this activity, tell them you will employ the "Round Table Strategy" as participants in grade-level cluster groups share successful product assignments they have used with students in their classrooms. Provide the following directions for this activity.

Round Table Strategy

- Instruct each group to have one piece of paper. That's right: one sheet per group.
- Ask *each* group member to take out a pen or pencil.
- Have the person who is the shortest in height among the group raise his or her hand. This person will go first by inputting information on the group paper. Then, they will rotate the paper clockwise.
- Tell the groups that the designated first person will write down *one product that that person has assigned (or will assign), observed, or read about for any unit of study* or lesson. After the one product is written down, the paper is passed clockwise and the next person writes down another product assigned in the classroom.

- Each group member continues to pass the paper around clockwise, adding a product used in the classroom.
- Tell participants that no duplications are allowed, so they should read all the previous entries before writing. Any participant is entitled to "pass" if all product ideas have been exhausted.
- You might set a time limit for this activity.
- After each group has finished its list and no one else can enter a line item, have a spokesperson from each group share the group's items. To do this, have a piece of butcher paper and write down what each group contributes. Ask groups to pay close attention so duplication is avoided. In an effort to expedite sharing, instruct each group to share two products at a time.
- Once the butcher paper is filled, distribute "Products." As a group, compare your lists to the provided list of sample formats for products. Discuss those formats that are unfamiliar or especially intriguing to participants. Once again, focus on the ability of a product to reveal student acquisition of concepts and principles in addition to knowledge and skill.

Teaching and Learning Activities

- Remind participants of the tenets of the Core Curriculum Parallel: *It establishes a rich framework of knowledge, understanding, and skills most relevant to the discipline.* Distribute "Flying Physics Product" and ask participants to provide evidence that this assignment was or was not designed to fit the goals of the Core Curriculum Parallel. (Note that without the checklist provided by the teacher, the assignment may not adequately address the intents of the Core Curriculum.)
- Ask participants to create or refine product assignments for their unit. Distribute "Product Suggestions for the Core Curriculum Parallel" to help them with this process. Emphasize how the products they design must provide evidence of *understanding* and not just knowledge and skill.

Closure/Looking Forward

Distribute "Matching Products to Core." Ask participants to use this handout to help them critique their own and their colleagues' product assignments. Remind them that they must be able to point out the way(s) in which the product assignments support the goals of the Core Curriculum.

PRODUCTS

Definition

Products are performances or work samples created by students that provide evidence of student understanding and learning. Products can represent daily or short-term student learning, or they can provide longer-term culminating evidence of student knowledge, understanding, and skill. High-quality products often double as assessment tools.

Characteristics

Powerful products are authentic, equitable, respectful, efficient, aligned to standards, and diagnostic. They should be used to measure student growth over time, to monitor and adjust instruction in order to promote student success, and as a basis for evaluating how well students can explain, interpret, apply, and transfer the essential content that has been identified in the unit.

Sample Formats

Advance organizer	Dance	Investment portfolio	Picture book	Skit
Advertisement	Debate	Journal	Picture dictionary	Slide presentation
Animation	Diagram	Lecture	Play	Small-scale model
Annotated bibliography	Diary	Lesson	Podcast	Social action plan
Argument	Dictionary	Letter	Poem	Song
Art work	Diorama	List	Portfolio	Sonnet
Assignment	Display	Log	Poster	Stencil
Audiotape	Dramatic monologue	Magazine article	PowerPoint presentation	Summary
Biography	Drawing	Map	Prediction	Survey
Blog	Economic forecast	Memoir	Protocol	Table or Graph
Blueprint	Editorial	Memorial	Proposal	Terrarium
Board game	Essay	Movie	Puppet	Textbook
Book jacket	Etching	Museum exhibit	Puppet show	Theory
Bulleted list	Experiment	Musical composition	Questions	Think piece
Bulletin board	Fable	Newspaper	Radio show	Timeline
Calendar	Fairy tale	Observation log	Relief map	TV newscast
Campaign	Family tree	Oral history	Reflection	Video game
Census	Filmstrip	Oral report	Research report	Video portfolio
Character sketch	Glossary	Outline	Rule	Vocabulary list
Chart	Graph	Overhead transparency	Science-fiction story	Web page
Choral reading	Graphic organizer	Pamphlet	Scrapbook	Web site
Chronology	Greeting card	Pantomime	Sculpture	Worksheet
Collage	Hypothesis	Paragraph	Set design	
Collection	Illustrated story	Pattern	Short story	
Comic strip	Interview	Photo essay	Simulation	
Compact disc	Fact file	Notes	Reader response	TV documentary
Critique	Invention	Photo journal		

Adapted from *The Parallel Curriculum* (Tomlinson, et al., 2008) Figure 3.2.

PRODUCT SUGGESTIONS FOR THE CORE CURRICULUM PARALLEL

- Ask students to create products that reflect their inquiry and analysis work.
- Assign concept maps to analyze the acquisition of concepts and principles.
- Ask students to make predictions, explain patterns, and demonstrate the relationship between raw data and primary source information and the core concepts and principles in the discipline.
- Ask students to demonstrate connections between unit activities and experiences and the concepts and principles in the discipline. Reflective essays, journal entries, charts, diagrams, and collages may support this task.
- Provide graphic organizers that allow students to communicate their acquisition of concepts, principles, and skills.

Adapted from *The Parallel Curriculum* (Tomlinson, et al., 2008) Figure 4.2.

FLYING PHYSICS PROJECT

You will complete a project that shows your understanding of our previous unit on "Motion" and our current unit on "Forces." Specifically, I want you to demonstrate that you are knowledgeable about how unbalanced forces cause changes in velocity. To show your understanding, you will create a project of your choice from the sheet titled "Flying Physics Project Choices." Any project you choose must include the items on the checklist below to fully satisfy this project.

- ❏ I clearly explain the difference between velocity and speed and show an example of each. I include math examples, as appropriate.
- ❏ I clearly explain the four forces of flight and how they interact.
- ❏ I draw or provide photographs for each of the major parts of the airplane that are involved in each of the four forces of flight. Each part is accompanied by a caption that explains the function.
- ❏ I include a definition and pictures to explain Bernoulli's Principle and its application to this project.
- ❏ I provide a thorough and complete explanation that accounts for why the same forces that keep a 747 flying also keep the airplane I built up and going.
- ❏ I provide at least two examples of two pairs of unbalanced forces interacting to produce movement.
- ❏ I use the language of the discipline in my explanations. I have checked all of my facts.
- ❏ My writing is typed and includes proper grammar and conventions (e.g., periods, capitalization, spelling, punctuation, indenting).
- ❏ My artwork/graphics are colorful (as appropriate), detailed, creative, and neat.
- ❏ My writing is organized in a way that makes sense, and all of my main points are clearly identified by subheadings and titles.
- ❏ My project has an appropriate title and my name/class period.
- ❏ It is obvious that I have done my personal best.

Flying Physics Product Choices

To display your information, you may choose one of the project choices below.

Project Cube or Mobile

Create a project cube by using a mailing box with six sides.
Cover the entire box with butcher paper to prepare it for this project.
Fill each side of the cube (except the top) with information that is detailed in the "Project Checklist." Your finished cube should have a consistent look to it. For instance, you might draw the same symbols, types of pictures, and/or colors on all sides to give it a cohesive look.

iMovie, PowerPoint, or Slide Show

Use technology to create your project. It must include all the information required on the "Project Checklist." Time limit: three minutes.

Picture Poster or Photo Journal

Create a picture poster or photo journal in which you include all the information required on the "Project Checklist." Create a layout first and then use it as your guide before putting your work on the poster paper or in the journal.

Comic Book, Brochure, or Magazine

Create a comic book, brochure, or magazine that includes all the information required on the "Project Checklist." Use a published comic book, brochure, or magazine as your guide for a layout. Make your work as professional as you can.

Song

Create lyrics to a song that includes all the information required on the "Project Checklist." You might create a song from scratch by making up the melody and lyrics, or you might create lyrics to a familiar tune. Share your song with the class by performing live or prerecording on audio- or videotape. If you play an instrument, you may use it as you sing. If your instrument is a clarinet or saxophone or something with a mouthpiece, prerecord the music and sing the song live with this accompanying instrumental recording. The song should have a chorus and at least three verses. Turn in a typed sheet of lyrics. Time limit: three minutes.

MATCHING PRODUCTS TO CORE

Your answers to the following questions (modified from the driving questions of the Core Curriculum) will help you ensure that the learning activities you incorporate into your unit are in sync with the intent and purposes of the Core Curriculum Parallel.

In what ways do your products:

- Maintain a focus on unit concepts and principles?
- Allow students to demonstrate unit knowledge and skills?
- Respond to differences in students' interests, learning preferences, and readiness levels?

WORKSHOP #12

Extension Activities Component of a Core Curriculum Unit

Session Overview

In this workshop, participants will design or remodel extension activities that serve to support the intent and purposes of unit goals and the Core Curriculum Parallel, and will extend unit goals.

Masters

- Extension Activities
- Health Unit Extensions
- Planning Extension Activities
- Matching Extensions to Core

Session Details

Introduction

- Ask participants to share what they think of when they hear the term *extension activity*. Ask why extension activities are useful and who might benefit from them. (Be sure they don't restrict the usefulness to advanced students. Any student with specific interests in a unit topic could also benefit from appropriately designed extensions.)
- Distribute and/or display "Extension Activities"

Teaching and Learning Activities

Say: "Within the Core Curriculum, extension activities can be used effectively to provide opportunities to learn additional information, examples, concepts, principles, skills, and applications not addressed in the basic Core Curriculum plan. By helping students develop extension activities, investigations, or products that reinforce and extend these key concepts, principles, and skills of the core curriculum, teachers can attend to both student curiosity and content goals."

Ask: "What are potential pitfalls in designing and carrying out extension activities in a unit of study?"

- If it has not surfaced during discussion, make the point that possible pitfalls are those activities that do not represent clear linkages to the learning goals or activities that are merely busywork. Extensions are often most useful when a student has some say in designing the activity.
- Share "Health Unit Extensions." Explain that the first column lists knowledge categories. The second column lists the unit's essential knowledge in those categories. The third column illustrates some ideas for extending student learning as student interest evolves.

Ask: "What about these extensions make them *extensions,* make them *high-quality extensions,* make them *core extensions*?"

- Share "Planning Extension Activities." Ask participants to use the questions on this handout to help them design or refine extension activities for their targeted unit. Remind them that they are developing extension activities, investigations, or products that reinforce and extend the key concepts, principles, and skills of the Core Curriculum Parallel. It may help them to have a specific student or group of students in mind as they design possible extensions for their unit.

Closure/Looking Forward

End the session by distributing "Matching Extensions to Core." Ask participants to critique each others' work, evaluating the degree to which their extensions match the intents and purposes of the Core Curriculum and/or provide expanded opportunities to address the driving questions of the Core Curriculum.

EXTENSION ACTIVITIES

Definition

Extension activities are preplanned or serendipitous experiences for individuals, small groups, or the entire class that emerge from learning goals, local events, and students' interests.

Characteristics

Powerful extension activities provide for student choice. They relate in some way to the content/standards, are open-ended and authentic, and generate excitement for and investment in learning. They may be of short duration or may require more extensive time.

High-Quality Extension Activities Help Students . . .

- Learn about related topics
- Explore or expand their interests
- Link a unit to current and/or historical events
- Explore career opportunities
- Transfer or apply new learning
- Solve a related problem
- Share a personal experience

Adapted from *The Parallel Curriculum* (Tomlinson, et al., 2008) Figure 3.2.

HEALTH UNIT EXTENSIONS

Subject Area: HEALTH	Grade 8 Concept: VIOLENCE		Disciplines: Psychology, Sociology	
Knowledge Categories	Essential Knowledge		Potential Extensions	
Facts	• Risk factors associated with violence • Situations that lead to fights		Myths versus facts about the causes and frequency of violence	
Concepts	• Victim • Assailant • Resolution • Hostility • Free-floating anger	• Violence • Mediation • Escalation	Learn more about: • Confrontation • Gangs • Instigator • Micro-insults	• Negotiation • Fight or fligh • De-escalation • Risk factors
Principles	• Violence is often perpetrated by people who have had personal contact with the victim • Poverty is more highly correlated with violence than is ethnicity		• The relationship between access to various weapons, especially, guns is correlated to incidence of violent crimes • Frustration and hopelessness may increase violence	
Skills	• Conflict resolution skills • Conflict mediation strategies		• Developing advice for students about how to deal with a bully • Investigating nonviolence in popular music	
Applications	• Logging violence on television • Interviewing people about their experiences with violence		• Analyzing violence in popular music • Analyzing domestic violence statistics in your town	

Adapted from *The Parallel Curriculum* (Tomlinson, et al., 2002) Figure 4.8.

PLANNING EXTENSION ACTIVITIES

To Think About

- Where can you find ideas for extension activities that can be used in your classroom?
- What resources might you tap in a search for adult role models of inquiry and research, primary source documents, field study opportunities, and real-world problems that relate to the core knowledge in the unit or discipline?
- What supplementary technology related to core knowledge (e.g., videos, CDs, software) might be available?
- How might you organize these extension activities for students? (e.g., learning centers, independent projects, anchor activities)
- What makes an extension interesting to students?
- Would all students find the extension activities interesting and/or useful?
- How might extension activities respond to differences in student readiness levels, interests, and learning preferences?

Adapted from *The Parallel Curriculum* (Tomlinson, et al., 2008) Figure 4.2.

MATCHING EXTENSIONS TO CORE

Your answers to the following questions (modified from the driving questions of the Core Curriculum) will help you ensure that the extensions you incorporate into your unit are in sync with the intent and purposes of the Core Curriculum Parallel.

Do the extension activities:

- Stem from or relate back to the *key concepts* and *principles* of the unit?
- Offer students the opportunity to add additional skills or knowledge about unit topics and/or the discipline?
- Connect to specific student interests and/or talents?

WORKSHOP #13

Differentiation and AID Component for the Core Curriculum Parallel

Note to Facilitator

To prepare for this workshop, you may wish to review Chapter 8, "Ascending Intellectual Demand in the Parallel Curriculum Model" in *The Parallel Curriculum* (Tomlinson, et al., 2008).

Session Overview

In this workshop, participants will modify their Core Curriculum unit content, activities, and/or product assignments to better meet varied student needs. Participants also will learn about and practice a type of differentiation specific to the Parallel Curriculum Model: *Ascending Intellectual Demand* (AID).

(Continued)

(Continued)

Masters

- Differentiation Based on Learner Need
- Fractions Projects
- Ascending Intellectual Demand
- Traits and Skills of Experts
- Novice to Expert Continuums
- AID and the Core Curriculum Parallel
- Matching Differentiation and AID to Core

Session Details

Introduction

- Assess participants' understanding and knowledge of differentiated instruction. To do this, you can hold an informal discussion in which participants share their experiences with it. Or you can have participants hold up one, two, or three fingers to indicate their level of understanding: one finger indicates no knowledge of differentiation; two fingers reflect some knowledge and maybe some experience with trying differentiation in the classroom; and three represent thorough understanding and successful implementation of differentiation on a regular basis.
- Ask participants to work in small groups to define the term *differentiation* and then share the definitions in the large group.
- Solicit examples of successful differentiation that they have carried out or seen carried out in the classroom. Make a list of characteristics of high-quality differentiation.
- Conduct the following small group activity.
  o Arrange participants in small groups. Provide each group with chart paper and markers.
  o Assign each group two of the following: preassessment, resources, teaching methods, learning activities, grouping format, products, rubrics, pacing, extension activities, learning goals.
  o With their assigned topics, have participants discuss and then record ideas on chart paper, design a visual, or provide examples that show how modifications might be made in order to better match student variance in readiness, interest, and learning preferences. Have each group share their results with the whole group.
- Distribute and discuss "Differentiation Based on Learner Need."

Teaching and Learning Activities

- Share "Fractions Projects" as an example of project choices that teachers might assign to elementary students who have scored high on a fractions preassessment. In lieu of some classroom teacher-directed activities in which they had already shown mastery, students would work on a project of interest from the four choices provided.
- Ask teachers to brainstorm ways they might support learners who struggle in a unit on fractions and how they might adapt fraction unit activities to respond to varied student interests and/or learning preferences.
- Ask teachers to discuss ways they might differentiate their own unit. Have them sketch out ideas for now and explain that they will have additional time to flesh out these ideas after you present information about a kind of differentiation called Ascending Intellectual Demand or AID.
- Share "Ascending Intellectual Demand."

Explain: "Ascending Intellectual Demand (AID) is a type of differentiation unique to the Parallel Curriculum Model. The goal of AID replicates the goal of an excellent coach who: (1) maps the growth of an athlete; (2) presents and supports opportunities to develop competencies at even higher levels of expertise; (3) helps the young person continually develop his or her capacity, sense of self-efficacy, and readiness as an athlete to test and hone skills at increasing levels of proficiency. AID provides a way of consistently and purposefully refining the match between learner development and curriculum and instruction so that all learners move along a continuum toward expertise in one or more disciplinary areas.

"To apply AID is to guide all young learners to walk increasingly in the paths of experts. Though there is some overlap between differentiation and AID, remember that the focus of AID is to ask students to work in ways that lead to increasing expertise in a discipline either as a practitioner or scholar."

- Ask participants to work in small groups to brainstorm a list of characteristics of expert teachers. Next ask them to make a list of characteristic of experts in general or of experts in their own discipline (historian, writer, musician, and so on). Distribute "Traits and Skills of Experts" and compare their ideas to those on the handout.
- Distribute "Novice to Expert Continuums." Ask participants to envision several of their most advanced students and decide where they think these students fall on this continuum with respect to their discipline. Point out the bidirectional arrows that connect each stage on the AID continuum. Remind participants that growth is not necessarily linear. In fact, it is quite common for a learner to be a novice in one aspect and an apprentice in another. Tell them the teacher response chart is designed to help them to think about ways to move even the most advanced students to the next level of expertise.
- Distribute "AID and the Core Curriculum Parallel." Ask participants to choose one or more components of their unit and differentiate for learner variance and/or ascending intellectual demand.

Closure/Looking Forward

End the session by distributing "Matching Differentiation and AID to Core." Ask participants to critique each others' work, evaluating the degree to which their differentiation choices match the intents and purposes of the Core Curriculum and/or provide expanded opportunities to address the driving questions of the Core Curriculum.

DIFFERENTIATION BASED ON LEARNER NEED

Definition

Teachers can enhance learning by optimizing the match between the curriculum and students' unique learning needs.

Characteristics

Well-designed differentiation strategies are closely aligned with the learning goals, research, assessment data, students' prior knowledge, cognitive skills, motivation, interests, learning modes, questions, and product preferences. Differentiation is designed for all levels of learners. It can mean giving additional support in following directions, for example, but it can also mean using more challenging texts for students who have strong reading skills. The goal is to modify those curricular elements that encourage each student to learn as much as possible and as efficiently and effectively as possible.

Sample Strategies

- Conduct small group sessions that (1) reteach topics or skills for students who have difficulty mastering them and/or (2) help advanced learners refine and expand their advanced knowledge and skills.
- Provide audiotapes of readings and/or an outline of the unit for students who have difficulty reading the textbook alone or who are highly auditory learners.
- Supplement oral presentations with overhead transparencies, a choice of advance organizers, and opportunities for small group discussions of content.
- Vary the amount of support offered to students during various tasks based on their individual needs.
- Offer students a choice of working alone or with partners, when appropriate.
- Set up the classroom so that students sometimes have the freedom to choose where to sit, what surfaces to work on, and with which materials they want to work.
- Maintain centers on topics of interest to learners.

Adapted from *The Parallel Curriculum* (Tomlinson, et al., 2008) Figure 3.2.

FRACTIONS PROJECTS

Learning Center

Create a learning center that your teacher can use to teach other students about fractions. The learning center you create must include:

- Fun, hands-on fractions activities that help players understand what fractions are, how fractions are used, and why they are important (no worksheets allowed)
- Answer key for any questions or problems
- Various levels of fractions activities from easy to more challenging
- Accurate, easy-to-follow directions (typed or neatly written)

Your center must be inviting for students. That means that the activities are fun and the center itself is colorful and creative. Plan your center and share this plan with your teacher. Once your teacher approves your idea, you can get started!

Game

Create a game incorporating fractions. The game can be about anything you are interested in as long as it helps players understand what fractions are, how fractions are used, and why they are important. Your game needs to have the following.

- A creative, eye-catching game board
- Directions
- Game strategy
- Anything else that is important to play your game

First, plan out your game board and then meet with your teacher to share your ideas. Once you get approval from your teacher, go for it! Other students may want to play your game. Make sure that players of your game will come away with a *better knowledge, understanding, and skill with fractions.*

Short Story

Write a short story using fractions as characters. Your story can be as creative and outlandish (far out) as you want, but it must include evidence that *you know what fractions are, how they are used, and why they are important.* Include a setting so your reader feels like she or he can see the places you have written about. Your story should include a beginning, middle, and end. It can be typed or neatly handwritten. Remember to include a title and illustrations, and brainstorm before you begin writing.

Song

Create lyrics to a song that focuses on fractions and teach the song to the class. The song must explain *what fractions are, how they are used, and why they are important.* You might create a song from scratch by making up the melody *and* lyrics, or you might create lyrics to a familiar tune. If you play an instrument, you may use it as you sing, unless you play an instrument such as a clarinet or saxophone. In that case, you may wish to record the music and sing along to the recording when you share your work. Your song should have a chorus and at least three verses. Neatly write or type your lyrics for your teacher so copies can be made for the class to use as you teach the song. Remember to brainstorm before writing. (Optional: Record the song on audiotape or videotape and share it with the class.)

ASCENDING INTELLECTUAL DEMAND

Definition

One kind of modification represented in the Parallel Curriculum Model is referred to as Ascending Intellectual Demand (AID). Some learners will advance quickly, developing the knowledge, skills, and dispositions necessary for work beyond their current stage. Other learners will make slow and steady progress through each stage over a longer period. The goal of AID is to develop knowledge, understanding, skills, and dispositions associated with expertise in all learners. Expertise is developed over time with careful attention to balancing appropriate levels of challenge, and support is highly personalized to the learner and should be based on a teacher's continual assessment of the learner at each stage of the continuum to determine learner characteristics, learner needs, and the most efficient and effective instructional responses.

TRAITS AND SKILLS OF EXPERTS

Traits/Attitudes of the Expert	Skills of the Expert
• High curiosity, reflection, concentration • Understands domain at a deep level • Uses present knowledge to plan for future directions in learning • Raises questions about reasons for and use of knowledge • Spends time to lay foundation, understand contexts and problems • Seeks out multiple resources and knows how to use them • Demonstrates high level of skill that looks effortless • Can mentally represent a problem and its parameters • Transforms content to use in new areas • Reflective, evaluative behavior • Makes great number of connections and more complex connections • Sensitive to task demands when solving problems • Has confidence in ability to solve problems • Examines impact of decisions on self, others, and society • Self-monitoring • Able to step outside personal experience • Insightful • Open-minded • Tolerates risk and uncertainty • Assumes responsibility for own learning • Driven to work hard • Inspires self to work • Disciplined approach to work • Continues to push for improvement • Incorporates struggle and failure in the journey to learn • Chooses to learn from experience • Seeks meaningful practice and critique • Has a commitment to excellence • Leads others to productive accomplishment • Envisions new possibilities	• Organizes knowledge for meaning and accessibility • Maintains an internal organization and has a classification system • Represents problems in a qualitatively deeper way • Transfers content and skills from one context to use in another • Sees differences between typical and novel instances • Has fast, accurate pattern recognition • Reflects on adequacy of own thinking processes • Anticipates sequences in learning • Poses insightful questions about content and problems • Can recount and evaluate events and their impact • Anticipates problems • Uses efficient methods of reflection and problem solving • Uses efficient pattern recognition to apply prior knowledge to new situations • Develops systems and habits for effective, efficient learning • Searches for subtle examples and information • Gleans pertinent information from seemingly extraneous data • Has a heuristic rather than a formulaic approach to solving problems • Works at high level of abstract, analytical, and creative thinking • Works at level of automaticity • Flexibly adapts parameters to facilitate purposes • Engages others in reflective, insightful dialogue • Creates novel products and applications

Source: Adapted from *The Parallel Curriculum* (Tomlinson, et al., 2008) Figure 4.8.

Experts in General

Ascending Intellectual Demand

Novice

- Experiences content at a concrete level
- Manipulates microconcepts one at a time
- Needs skill instruction and guided practice
- Requires support, encouragement, and guidance
- Seeks affirmation of competency in order to complete a task

Knowledge | Skills
Attitudes | Habits of Mind

Apprentice

- Understands the connections among microconcepts within a discipline
- Connects information within a microconcept
- Begins to interpret generalizations and themes that connect concepts
- Applies skills with limited supervision
- Seeks confirmation at the end of a task
- Reflects upon content and skills when prompted

Knowledge | Skills
Attitudes | Habits of Mind

Practitioner

- Manipulates two or more microconcepts simultaneously
- Creates generalizations that explain connections among concepts
- Selects and uses skills in order to complete a task
- Seeks input from others as needed
- Exhibits task commitment and persistence when challenges are moderate
- Reflects upon both content and skills in order to improve understanding/performance

Knowledge | Skills
Attitudes | Habits of Mind

Expert

- Uses concepts within and among disciplines in order to derive theories and principles
- Creates innovations within a field
- Practices skill development independently and for the purpose of improvement
- Seeks input from other experts in a field for a specific purpose
- Works to achieve flow and derives pleasure from the experience (high challenge, advanced skill/knowledge)
- Is independent and self-directed as a learner
- Seeks experiences that cause a return to previous levels in varying degrees

Knowledge | Skills
Attitudes | Habits of Mind

(Continued)

(Continued)

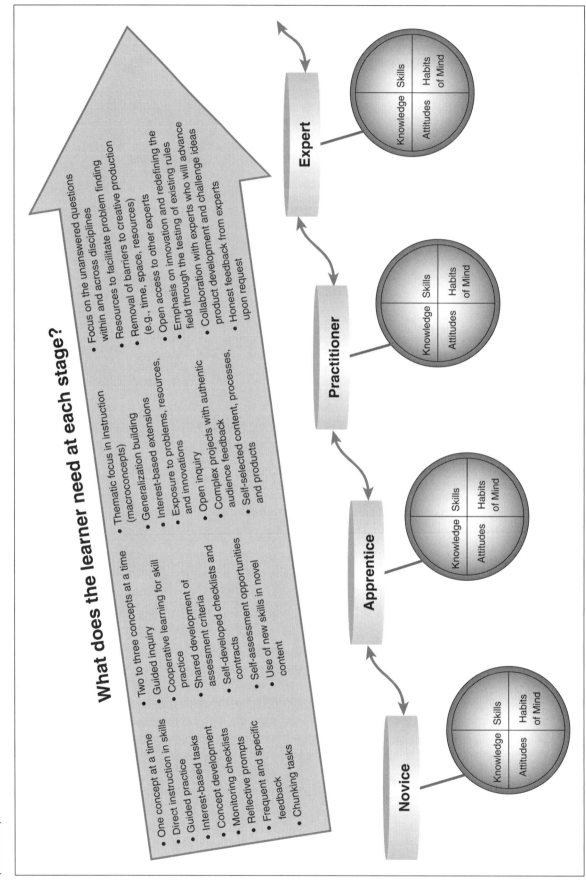

What does the learner need at each stage?

- One concept at a time
- Direct instruction in skills
- Guided practice
- Interest-based tasks
- Concept development
- Monitoring checklists
- Reflective prompts
- Frequent and specific feedback
- Chunking tasks

- Two to three concepts at a time
- Guided inquiry
- Cooperative learning for skill practice
- Shared development of assessment criteria
- Self-developed checklists and contracts
- Self-assessment opportunities
- Use of new skills in novel content

- Thematic focus in instruction (macroconcepts)
- Generalization building
- Interest-based extensions
- Exposure to problems, resources, and innovations
- Open inquiry
- Complex projects with authentic audience feedback
- Self-selected content, processes, and products

- Focus on the unanswered questions within and across disciplines
- Resources to facilitate creative production
- Removal of barriers to creative production (e.g., time, space, resources)
- Open access to other experts
- Emphasis on innovation and redefining the field through the testing of existing rules who will advance ideas
- Collaboration with experts and challenge ideas product development
- Honest feedback from experts upon request

Novice — Apprentice — Practitioner — Expert

(Each stage circle divided into: Knowledge | Skills / Attitudes | Habits of Mind)

Experts in Sample Content Areas

The Expert in English and Language Arts	*The Expert in Science*
• Demonstrates knowledge, reflection, creativity, and critical analysis of language arts skills and concepts across a wide variety of disciplines • Applies the wide range of skills associated with effective oral and written communication, reading, and research with automaticity • Reading, writing, speaking, and researching lead to personal fulfillment beyond the goals of learning and the exchange of information • Appreciates the power of the written and spoken word • Questions the accepted conventions and rules • Experiments with methods to communicate and develop greater understanding • Practices in all areas (i.e., written and oral communication, reading, and research)	• Demonstrates automaticity with the tools and process skills in scientific research and investigation • Clearly links explanation to current scientific knowledge, pushing the field forward by extending the body of knowledge • Poses original scientific questions that test the limits of the existing body of knowledge in a field • Seeks and derives satisfaction from the ambiguous situations in science • Demonstrates persistence despite personal and professional obstacles • Has a sense of needing to know the answer as a driving force to engage in continuous research • Seeks to make a contribution to the discipline and or field (e.g., new experiments, new observations, new methods and tools, new theories, principles, and rules) • Conducts complex experiments with ease and fluidity, freely manipulates methods, tools knowledge, and self to achieve desired results • Seeks interaction with other experts for purposes of ideas clarification, new ideas, and research • Identifies error in their own research and problem-solves to minimize error • Invites constructive criticism by publishing findings from research studies in scientific journals, participation in symposiums, conferences, and seminars • Proposes theories open to review once sufficient evidence is gathered, organized, and analyzed • Collaborates with fellow scientists for the purposes of critical analysis, refinement of ideas, and to push the existing body of knowledge in field forward

(Continued)

(Continued)

The Expert in Math	The Expert in History
• Uses computation as merely a means to an end • Questions existing mathematical principles • Moves easily among the fields of mathematics through the use of macroconcepts • Links mathematical principles to other fields through real-world problems • Seeks the challenge of unresolved problems and the testing of existing theories • Seeks flow through the manipulation of tools and methods in complex problem solving • Views unanswered questions in other disciplines through the concepts of mathematics • Uses reflection and practice as tools for self-improvement	• Moves easily from the theoretical to the practical and vice versa in response to a situation • Challenges accepted bodies of knowledge, methods, and research findings • Develops themes and connections across historical events, periods, and fields without reliance, but with acknowledgement of chronology • Uses the knowledge and skills of the discipline across diverse fields and disciplines • Displays curiosity and seeks challenge through unanswered questions in the field • Marvels at the richness of history and its importance in shaping the present and future • Systematically and with automaticity uses the knowledge, skills, and processes of the discipline to investigate

Adapted from *The Parallel Curriculum* (Tomlinson, et al., 2008) Figures 8.13, 8.25, 8.37, and 8.49.

AID AND THE CORE CURRICULUM PARALLEL

To promote AID:

- Use professional-level reading, resources, and research materials.
- Adjust the pace of teaching and learning.
- Ask students to discover, test, and defend the importance of key concepts and principles in the discipline.
- Design work at greater levels of depth, breadth, complexity, and/or abstractness.
- Require students to apply ideas and skills to contexts quite unfamiliar and dissimilar from applications explored in class.
- Design tasks that are more open-ended or ambiguous in nature and/or that call on students to exercise greater independence in thought and scholarly behavior as learners and producers.
- Develop rubrics for tasks and/or products that articulate levels of quality that include expert-level indicators.

- Encourage collaborations between students and adult experts in an area of shared interest.
- Design work that requires continuing student reflection on the significance of ideas and information and that causes students to generate new and useful ways to represent ideas and information.

Adapted from *The Parallel Curriculum* (Tomlinson, et al., 2008) Figure 4.9.

MATCHING DIFFERENTIATION AND AID TO CORE

Your answers to the following questions (modified from the driving questions of the Core Curriculum) will help you ensure that any differentiation you design remains in sync with the intent and purposes of the Core Curriculum Parallel.

Does the differentiation:

- Retain a clear focus on the *key concepts* and *principles* of the unit?
- Feel respectful? In other words, are differentiated options equally challenging and equally engaging to the students for whom they are designed?

Do AID opportunities:

- Retain a clear focus on the *key concepts* and *principles* of the unit?
- Acknowledge the current level of student expertise and help students work toward an even more advanced level of expertise in a discipline?

WORKSHOP #14

Closure Component for the Core Curriculum Parallel

Session Overview

In this workshop, participants will design closure activities for their unit that match the intents and purposes of the Core Curriculum Parallel.

Masters

- Closure
- Matching Closure to Core

Session Details

Introduction

Say: "Despite our best efforts at clarity and coherence, some students may still walk away from the classroom with varied conclusions—or no conclusions about the point of the lesson and/or unit. An effective lesson closure enables the teacher to focus student attention on what matters most in the unit and on the ways in which the lesson or unit content relates to the discipline in general as well as to their own lives and interests.

(Continued)

(Continued)

Ask: "How do you typically end a lesson? A unit?" What makes your current closure activities successful? What would you like to change or refine?

Teaching and Learning Activities

- Distribute "Closure." Tell participants that virtually any learning activity can serve as closure as long as that activity leads to a sense of finishing a learning process or a significant step along the way. Teachers should build in a short closure activity to every class period, but closure is particularly important at the end of a lesson or unit of study.
- Ask participants to design an appropriate closure activity for their unit. Remind them that in a Core Curriculum unit, it is important that closure activities focus on the meaning of the unit's concepts, principles, and skills as well as its associated activities.

Closure/Looking Forward

End the session by distributing "Matching Closure to Core." Ask participants to critique each others' work, evaluating the degree to which their closure activities match the intents and purposes of the Core Curriculum and/or provide expanded opportunities to address the driving questions of the Core Curriculum.

CLOSURE

Definition

Lesson and unit closure allows for reflection on the "punch line" of the lesson. What was the point of the lesson? What are students taking away from it? What questions remain? What comes next?

Characteristics

Effective lesson and unit closure helps students solidify their understanding of how their studies make sense, how the ideas and skills can be used, and why they matter. Closure provides a satisfying end to a learning experience.

Sample Strategies

- Whole or small group discussion
- Individual reflection or journal writing
- Exit cards
- Graphic organizers
- Analogies
- Stories
- Summarization activities
- Review of lesson or unit goals
- Asking students to state the point of the lesson or unit
- Revisiting introductory activities.

Adapted from *The Parallel Curriculum* (Tomlinson, et al., 2008) Figure 3.2.

MATCHING CLOSURE TO CORE

Your answers to the following questions (modified from the driving questions of the Core Curriculum) will help you ensure that your closure activities remain in sync with the intent and purposes of the Core Curriculum Parallel.

Closure activities in a Core Unit should help students answer the following questions:

- What does the information in this unit mean to me? To scholars and practitioners of the discipline?
- Why does this information matter?
- What are these ideas and skills for? How can I use them?
- How does this information fit in the grand scheme of the discipline? Of life?

Note to Facilitator

Before you move participants onto Chapter 3 of this book, "The Curriculum of Connections," discuss with your group how much curriculum sharing they wish to do. If you have a varied group, they may wish to confine their sharing to grade/subject-alike groups. If it's a small group, you might suggest sitting in a circle and allowing each person to share. But leave it to the participants to determine whether they wish to share the work done as a result of this Core Curriculum Parallel chapter so that they have ownership over how their valuable time is spent.

Also gather input from participants about the logistics of previous sessions and what suggestions they might have for future sessions. For example, discuss organization of materials. Since people organize their work in different ways, it might be helpful to offer time for participants to share how they housed their work and whether they would recommend this method for subsequent sessions. Another discussion point you might suggest is the timing of the sessions. If there is flexibility, then open up dialogue centering on these questions:

- To what extent did the day of the week and the frequency with which we held these sessions work well?
- What is your feedback about the time of day these sessions were held?
- Discuss the frequency and timing of breaks, group activities, and uninterrupted time devoted to writing curriculum.

Finishing Chapters 1 and 2 is a milestone, so you might consider hosting a celebration to congratulate participants on a job well done.

The Curriculum of Connections Parallel

The Curriculum of Connections Parallel

To prepare for the workshops in this chapter, you may wish to review Chapter 3, "Thinking About the Elements of Curriculum Design," and Chapter 5, "The Curriculum of Connections Parallel" of *The Parallel Curriculum* by Tomlinson, et al., (2008).

Session Overview

This session focuses on the basic tenets of the Curriculum of Connections, specifically its definition, intent, benefits, and driving questions.

Masters

- Nuts and Bolts of the Curriculum of Connections Parallel
- Curriculum of Connections at Work in the Classroom
- Checklist for Designing Curriculum Within the Curriculum of Connections Parallel

Session Details

Introduction

- First, review with participants that there are four ways of approaching curriculum. Tell them the focus for this seminar is the Curriculum of Connections. Reintroduce the master titled "The Parallel Curriculum" (Workshop #1) and draw attention to the second parallel—the *Curriculum of Connections*. Since this parallel asks students to make connections within or across disciplines, across times, across cultures or places, or in some combination of those elements, pose these questions to participants to model questioning for this parallel:

  ○ How has thinking about curriculum evolved over the years?
  ○ How has your thinking about curriculum evolved from your first year of teaching to now?

o In terms of curriculum, what are some similarities and differences between the school you are teaching in now and another school in which you have taught?

o If you have taught in another country, what are some cultural similarities and differences in the curriculum that you have noticed?

o What connections can you make between students now and in the past?

- Explain that the focus for this next set of workshops is to directly apply what they learn about the Curriculum of Connections Parallel to remodel a chosen lesson(s) or unit to align with this parallel. Tell participants that the following sessions on this parallel are designed similarly to the ones on the Core Curriculum.

Teaching and Learning Activities

Say: "The Curriculum of Connections is derived from and extends the Core Curriculum Parallel. It is designed to help students encounter and interact with the key concepts, principles, and skills of a discipline in a variety of settings, times, and circumstances."

- Distribute and discuss "Nuts and Bolts of the Curriculum of Connections Parallel."
- Ask participants to first think about, then share in small groups, the answer to these questions:

o Why should we design curriculum that offers connections?

o When designing curriculum to help students make connections, what kind of connections to you tend to focus on—connections across time? Across space? Across disciplines?

o What other kinds of connections in the handout do you find intriguing?

o How is the Curriculum of Connections similar to and different from what we know as interdisciplinary teaching and/or intradisciplinary teaching?

Note to Facilitator: One common difference between the Curriculum of Connections and interdisciplinary or intradisciplinary instruction is the former's firm emphasis on concepts and principles. For more help with these distinctions, see pages 130–133 in *The Parallel Curriculum* (Tomlinson, et al., 2008).

- Share "Curriculum of Connections at Work in the Classroom." Ask participants to work with others at their grade level to discuss either the elementary or secondary example (or both). They should discuss ways in which these examples match the intent and purposes of the Curriculum of Connections and address its driving questions.

Ask the whole group: "In what ways are the intents and purposes of the Core Curriculum also represented in these examples?" (Remind participants that all Parallel Curriculum units reflect the principles of the Core Curriculum.)

- Participants' upcoming task is to remodel or create quality lessons for a unit of study with the Curriculum of Connections Parallel as the focus. Distribute "Checklist for Designing Curriculum Within the Curriculum of Connections Parallel." Ask participants to use the checklist to examine strengths and weaknesses of a unit of study from their own or their district's curriculum. Suggest that for this activity they choose a unit they know quite well. If they prefer, they might return to the unit they designed to match the Core Curriculum. This would ensure that they begin with a solid unit, and can focus on ways they might adapt the unit to fit the Curriculum of Connections.

Closure/Looking Forward

- In small groups and then whole group sharing, invite participants to make a list of the benefits that this parallel can offer teachers and students.
- Tell participants that the next sessions will focus on examining how the key components of curriculum might look in a Curriculum of Connections unit.
- Remind them of the symbol they developed in Workshop #1 to represent the Curriculum of Connections. Ask them if they wish to change or adapt this symbol.

NUTS AND BOLTS OF THE CURRICULUM OF CONNECTIONS PARALLEL

Intents/Purposes of the Curriculum of Connections

The Curriculum of Connections helps students:

- Use concepts, principles, and skills to see the interrelatedness of knowledge as experts do.
- Find key ideas in various contexts and examine their similarities and differences.
- Apply skills in varied settings.
- Use ideas from one context to ask questions about other situations.
- Use ideas from multiple settings to create new hypotheses.
- Make analogies between contexts.
- Develop ways to see unfamiliar things using familiar ways.
- Develop an appreciation for multiple perspectives on issues.
- Understand the role of individuals in the changes within a evolution of the discipline.

Driving Questions of the Curriculum of Connections

- What key concepts and principles have I learned?
- In what other contexts can I use what I have learned?
- How do the ideas and skills I have learned work in other contexts?
- How do I use the ideas and skills to develop insights or solve problems?
- How do different settings cause me to change or reinforce my earlier understandings?
- How do I adjust my way of thinking and working when I encounter new contexts?
- How do I know if my adjustments are effective?
- How does looking at one thing help me understand another?
- Why do different people have different perspectives on the same issue?
- How are perspectives shaped by time, place, culture, events, and circumstances?
- In what ways is it beneficial for me to examine varied perspectives on a problem or issue?
- How do I assess the relative strengths and weaknesses of differing viewpoints?
- What connections do I see between what I am studying and my own life and times?

Adapted from *The Parallel Curriculum* (Tomlinson, et al., 2008) Figure 5.2.

CURRICULUM OF CONNECTIONS AT WORK IN THE CLASSROOM

Secondary Example

In Mrs. Bernstein's history class, making connections is an ongoing emphasis for all students. Throughout the year, three concepts are used to organize the curriculum: culture, continuity, and diversity. At the end of the second quarter, all students will work with projects that ask them to use these concepts to compare their own culture with that of Russia. For this project, many students will select or develop a family that is similar to theirs but that lives in Russia. Students then show how the geography in which the two families live is alike and different. They will also show how aspects of culture, such as music, technology, religion, and jobs have changed for their own family and for the Russian family in the past twenty-five years.

In the end, they will write about ways in which continuity and diversity are evident in each culture over the past two-and-a-half decades. In addition to this project that helps them to see how culture, diversity, and continuity work across the cultures, each of the students will keep a journal that relates the three concepts to: (1) the students' other classes, and (2) the world around them (e.g., music, home, current events, movies, reading).

Elementary Example

Mrs. Gomez, Fourth Grade Science

Mrs. Gomez works with a group of fourth graders identified as gifted in science.

She meets with them three times a week for an hour each time in a class designed to extend their science curriculum. In this pull-out science class, she uses the Curriculum of Connections to help students link what they are learning in their regular classroom science curriculum to a broader set of understandings and applications. In their regular classroom, they have been studying the topic of weather.

Mrs. Gomez first worked with the students to help them see how weather is part of a "system." Students and teacher examined weather systems and other systems (e.g., family systems, the school as a system, and body systems) to propose statements they believed would be true about systems in general (principles). They then tested and refined the principles by looking at weather systems in their area.

Now Mrs. Gomez and her fourth graders are looking at connections between weather systems and ecosystems in several very different parts of the world (the Sahara Desert, Antarctica, and a South American rain forest). Their goal is to generate and test principles that would show the relationship between weather systems and ecosystems in general, and between weather systems and particular elements in ecosystems (animals, plants, rocks, and food chains). Students will gather data from a number of sources to test their hypotheses, work with the teacher to develop a systematic way of evaluating their data, and ultimately present a science newsletter that will be available online and in the library for other students to use as a resource in their study of weather. The newsletter will stress linkages between (1) the concept of systems as applied to weather systems and ecosystems and (2) the scientific processes of data gathering and analysis in understanding the linkages.

Mrs. Gomez took the topic-based classroom curriculum and helped her students look at it through a conceptual lens, stressing the key concept *system*. Then she used the Curriculum of Connections to help students generalize their knowledge and extend it through linkages made to unfamiliar geographic settings and two applications: weather systems and ecosystems—the former more familiar to the students and the latter less so.

Adapted from *The Parallel Curriculum* (Tomlinson, et al., 2002) pp. 26–28.

CHECKLIST FOR DESIGNING CURRICULUM WITHIN THE CURRICULUM OF CONNECTIONS PARALLEL

To what degree is the unit designed to help students think about and apply key concepts, principles, and skills:

- In a range of instances throughout the discipline?
- Across disciplines?
- Across time and time periods?

- Across locations?
- Across cultures?
- Across times, locations, and cultures?
- Through varied perspectives?
- As impacted by various conditions (e.g., social, economic, technological, political)?
- Through the eyes of various people who affected the ideas?
- By examining links between concepts and development of the disciplines?

Adapted from *The Parallel Curriculum* (Tomlinson, et al., 2008) Figure 2.1.

WORKSHOP #16

Content Component of a Curriculum of Connections Unit

Session Overview

In this workshop, participants will examine what the content component of curriculum might look like in a Curriculum of Connections unit. They also will work to design or revise their own unit content to match the intent and purposes of this parallel.

Masters

- Content Suggestions for the Curriculum of Connections
- Classroom Planning Examples

Session Details

Introduction

- Make sure participants have their tools for this seminar: district/state standards, lessons/unit to be taught and remodeled, appropriate textbooks and resources, and a laptop (optional).
- Display "Key Components of Comprehensive Curriculum" (Workshop #2). Place teachers in mixed subject or grade groups so they can benefit from a broad range of perspectives on this issue.

Say: "In your groups, review the components that are essential to planning a high-quality curriculum. What might each component (or assigned components) look like in a unit designed to match the intents and purposes of the Curriculum of Connections Parallel?" (You might not want to allow participants too much time brainstorming Curriculum of Connections ideas for each component since they will be delving into this work in-depth very soon. This is merely a springboard for the work they will do in designing or redesigning their own Curriculum of Connections unit.)

- Distribute "Content Suggestions for the Curriculum of Connections."

Teaching and Learning Activities

- For this parallel, suggest to participants that those who work on formalized interdisciplinary teams, teachers who service the same students and teach different subject areas, and self-contained teachers of the same grade level sit together. This would facilitate discussion on how they might connect instruction through a focus on common concepts, principles, skills, and dispositions, as well as overarching macroconcepts.

Say: "Knowing the standards and content of a unit is crucial to effective planning and teaching. When a teacher decides to create a Curriculum of Connections unit, the search for common concepts, or macroconcepts, across disciplines or topics is a good first step in the planning process."

- Share "Classroom Planning Examples" and discuss ways participants might use the templates in the examples to help them identify or choose content for a Curriculum of Connections unit.
- Provide time for participants to plan unit content that is aligned with the intents and purposes of the Curriculum of Connections.

Closure/Looking Forward

Ask participants to critique each others' work, evaluating the degree to which their unit content matches the intents and purposes of the Curriculum of Connections (see "Checklist for Designing Curriculum Within the Curriculum of Connections Parallel") and/or provides opportunities to address the driving questions of that parallel (see "Driving Questions of the Curriculum of Connections" in Appendix D).

CONTENT SUGGESTIONS FOR THE CURRICULUM OF CONNECTIONS

- Identify the units or topics you are assigned to teach.
- Identify the discipline(s) with which these topics are associated.
- Make a list of the major facts, concepts, principles, dispositions, and skills to be addressed in each unit of study.
- Consider the kinds of information students will learn—places, events, people, things, or characteristics. Identify analogous items in other topics, locations, time periods, fields, or disciplines.
- Consider the concepts that students will learn in this unit. Identify the use of similar concepts in other topics, fields, or disciplines.
- Consider the principles that students will learn in this unit. Identify analogous principles that explain relationships within other topics, fields, or disciplines.
- Consider the dispositions that students will address in this unit. Identify analogous dispositions in other situations, career areas, fields, or disciplines.
- Consider the skills that students will learn in this unit. Identify analogous skills needed to think, learn, investigate, or produce in other topic areas, fields, or disciplines.
- Consider working with colleagues who teach different subject areas to the same students. Discuss how you might connect two or more units of instruction through a focus on common concepts, principles, skills, and dispositions.

Adapted from *The Parallel Curriculum* (Tomlinson, et al., 2008) Figure 5.3.

CLASSROOM PLANNING EXAMPLES

Example 1

Complete column three with examples from a specific unit.

Knowledge Category	*Definitions/Examples*	*Your Unit Examples*
Macroconcepts (Interdisciplinary version of concepts)	A general idea or understanding, a generalized idea of a thing or a class of things; a category or classification that extends across disciplines *Examples:* • Form • Function • Systems • Change • Patterns • Conflict • Perspective • Interdependence	
Generalizations and Themes (Interdisciplinary version of principles)	A fundamental theme or generalization to explain the relationship between two or more concepts in two or more disciplines *Examples:* • Form follows function. • Our perspectives are shaped by and shape our experiences. • Change is painful. • Measure twice, cut once. • Parts of systems are interdependent.	
Interdisciplinary Processes	Proficiencies, abilities, techniques, strategies, methods, or tools that have multiple, interdisciplinary applications *Examples:* • Identifying patterns • Making deductive inferences • Observing • Making a plan • Solving a problem • Researching and communicating findings	
Interdisciplinary Dispositions	Beliefs, dispositions, appreciations, or values that transcend cultures, time, and disciplines *Examples:* • An appreciation for patience • A belief in the critical importance of empathy • An understanding of perspective • A positive attitude toward curiosity • Intrinsic motivation for learning	

Adapted from *The Parallel Curriculum* (Tomlinson, et al., 2008) Figure 5.4.

Example 2

Make and complete a grid similar to the one below.

Target Concepts (Social Studies)	Related Math Concepts	Related Science Concepts	Related Language Arts Concepts	Related Music Concepts	Related Art Concepts	Related Physical Education Concepts	INTERDISCIPLINARY MACROCONCEPTS
Culture		Species Biome System Habitat Niche	Genre	Form	Style		FORM
Transportation Immigration Emigration		Circulation Migration Transfer	Segues Storytelling		School Influence	Movement	MOVEMENT PROGRESSION CHANGE
Resources Needs	Variables	Survival Energy	Folktales		Subject Media		

- **Topical Principle:** Immigrants used various means of transportation to move from their homes and cultures to the United States to seek abundant resources and opportunities to improve their living conditions.
- **Discipline-Based Principle:** Throughout time, some individuals and subgroups within a culture have used available means of transportation to explore or resettle in other locations and regions in order to find or use new or additional resources or opportunities.
- **Interdisciplinary Generalization or Theme:** Living things, human products, and technology adapt, improve, or make progress as a result of movement.

Adapted from *The Parallel Curriculum* (Tomlinson, et al., 2008) Figure 5.6.

Example 3

Make and complete a grid similar to the one below.

Key Concepts Related to the Civil War	Topics, Events, Products, and People Related to the Study of the Civil War	Related Concepts From Other Topics, Subjects, or Disciplines	Related Topics, Events, Products, and People From Other Time Periods, Cultures, or Disciplines
Culture Perspective Time Period	Northern States Southern States Slave Culture	Culture Perspective Time Period	Taliban Regime Indian Reservation System Apartheid in South Africa The U.S. in the 1960s U.S. Women's Culture from 1820 to 1920

(Continued)

(Continued)

Key Concepts Related to the Civil War	Topics, Events, Products, and People Related to the Study of the Civil War	Related Concepts From Other Topics, Subjects, or Disciplines	Related Topics, Events, Products, and People From Other Time Periods, Cultures, or Disciplines
Labor Resources Goods and Services	Dred Scott Decision Frederick Douglass Factories Plantations Slave Trade Industrialization Slavery	Property Human Rights Civil Rights Immigration Prejudice	Child Labor Unionism Great Migration
Abolitionist Movement Emancipation	Harper's Ferry John Brown Sojourner Truth Harriet Tubman *Uncle Tom's Cabin* Harriet Beecher Stowe Levi Coffin Lucretia Mott Underground Railroad	Freedom Movements Trends Change Loss	The Suffrage Movement The Civil Rights Movement of the 1960s Women's Rights Movement Peace Movement Native American Movement Americans with Disabilities Movement War on Poverty Green Revolution Nationalism in South Africa
States' Rights Federalism Balance of Power	Secession Confederacy United States Westward Movement Territories	Colonialism Nationalism Balance of Power Independence	Bill of Rights British Colonies Ireland Branches of Government
Conflict Compromise Consensus Civil War/Unrest Resolution	Missouri Compromise Compromise of 1850 Fort Sumter Battle of Gettysburg Antietam Battle of Vicksburg Sherman's March Appomattox	Conflict Compromise Consensus Treaties Civil War/Unrest Revolution Revolt Demonstrations	Egypt-Israel Peace Accord Vietnam War Great Plains Wars Bosnia War Irish Conflict Indian Revolution
Leadership	Abraham Lincoln Jefferson Davis General Grant General Lee General Sherman Stonewall Jackson Henry Clay Nat Turner	Change Agents Leadership	Nelson Mandela Martin Luther King, Jr. Elizabeth Cady Stanton Betty Friedan Gloria Steinem Thurgood Marshall Mahatma Gandhi Susan B. Anthony

Adapted from *The Parallel Curriculum* (Tomlinson, et al., 2008) Figure 5.11.

Example 4: Step by Step Planner

- Identify the units or topics you are assigned to teach and the discipline(s) with which these topics are associated.
- Make a list of the major facts, concepts, principles, dispositions, and skills to be addressed in the unit of study. Identify analogous items in other topics, locations, periods, fields, or disciplines.
- Consider the kinds of information students will learn—places, events, people, things, or characteristics. Identify analogous items in other topics, locations, periods, fields, or disciplines.
- Consider working with colleagues who teach different subject areas to the same students. Discuss how you might connect two or more units of instruction through a focus on common concepts, principles, skills, and dispositions.

WORKSHOP #17

Assessment Component of a Curriculum of Connections Unit

Session Overview

In this workshop, participants will examine what assessments activities might look like in Curriculum of Connections unit. They also will work to design or revise their own assessments to match the intent and purposes of this parallel.

Masters

- Assessment Suggestions for the Curriculum of Connections
- Rubric for Measuring the Attainment of a Macroconcept
- Rubric for Measuring the Acquisition of an Interdisciplinary Rule, Principle, or Generalization

Session Details

Introduction

- If necessary, review the definition and characteristics of assessment (Workshop #5). Ask participants what they would expect to see in assessments that are designed to fit a Curriculum of Connections unit. Ask how such assessments might differ from those designed for a Core Curriculum unit.
- Distribute and discuss: "Assessment Suggestions for the Curriculum of Connections."

Teaching and Learning Activities

Say: "A comparison of the assessment components for both the Core Curriculum and the Curriculum of Connections reveals subtle differences in both rubric design and assessment strategies. Rubrics for the Curriculum of Connections contain descriptors of increasing levels of student expertise as well as criteria related to students' ability to demonstrate knowledge of patterns, principles, and themes across topics, periods, and disciplines. Assessment for the Core Curriculum must be aligned with this purpose and allow students to communicate growth, over time, in their ability to see larger and broader classifications for facts, skills, concepts, principles, dispositions.

(Continued)

(Continued)

> "Rubrics that are designed for assessments in a Curriculum of Connections unit also will reflect the 'flavor' of that parallel. In addition to content specific descriptors, teachers are likely to include a measure of student expertise in making the kinds of connections on which this parallel is based."

- Distribute "Rubric for Measuring Attainment of a Macroconcept" and "Rubric for Measuring the Acquisition of an Interdisciplinary Rule, Principle, or Generalization" to provide examples of what descriptors might look like at various levels of expertise.
- Have participants create their own Curriculum of Connections assessments and accompanying rubrics, or refashion their Core Curriculum unit assessments to reflect the intents and purposes of the Curriculum of Connections.

Closure/Looking Forward

After assessments are complete, allow time for groups to share specific examples with one another and provide feedback. Encourage them to highlight how their work incorporates the unique qualities of the Curriculum of Connections (see "Checklist for Designing Curriculum Within the Curriculum of Connections Parallel") and/or provides opportunities to address the driving questions of that parallel (see "Driving Questions of the Curriculum of Connections" in Appendix D).

ASSESSMENT SUGGESTIONS FOR THE CURRICULUM OF CONNECTIONS

- Supply students with word banks that list major concepts and ask them to create concept maps that link related concepts and principles in one topic with those in another topic or discipline.
- Develop rubrics that address growth in the understanding of macroconcepts, processes, and generalizations across topics and disciplines.
- Provide preassessments to identify students' prior experiences with the discipline and the concepts and principles they have attained to date. Build on this knowledge in the upcoming unit through the use of synectics and metaphoric thinking.

RUBRIC FOR MEASURING THE ATTAINMENT OF A MACROCONCEPT

	Level of Understanding	*Examples*
Expert	When confronted with new information in another discipline, students attempt to classify the new information using an interdisciplinary macroconcept.	"The population in our small, rural town experienced a decline in the 2000 census. I wonder if migration is a factor."
Proficient	The learner can classify and name comparable concepts in two or more fields as macroconcepts.	"The concept of beneficial movement is evident in both biology and anthropology."

	Level of Understanding	Examples
Competent	The learner can identify commonalities between concepts in one field or topic and concepts in another field or discipline.	"The migration of whales has several things in common with the migration of human beings."
Developing	The learner can use the concept to categorize and understand new information in the same field or discipline.	"Migration is evident during the 1880s, the early 1900s, the 1930s, and the 1940s in various parts of the United States."
Beginning	The learner can define and provide key attributes that distinguish a concept in a given field or discipline.	"Migration is the purposeful movement of living things across regions."

Adapted from *The Parallel Curriculum* (Tomlinson, et al., 2008) Figure 5.7.

RUBRIC FOR MEASURING THE ACQUISITION OF AN INTERDISCIPLINARY RULE, PRINCIPLE, OR GENERALIZATION

	Level of Understanding
Expert	The learner searches for interdisciplinary themes or generalizations in unfamiliar information in order to identify analogous or equivalent situations and develop creative solutions to real-world problems.
Proficient	The learner searches for interdisciplinary themes or generalizations in unfamiliar information in order to identify analogous or equivalent situations.
Competent	The learner can use knowledge about principles in various disciplines or topics to develop an interdisciplinary theme or generalization.
Developing	The learner can provide novel examples of the principle, theme, or generalization across events, topics, field of study, or disciplines.
Beginning	The learner can identify and explain a principle or relationship within a topic or field of study.

Adapted from *The Parallel Curriculum* (Tomlinson, et al., 2008) Figure 5.8.

WORKSHOP #18

Introductory Activities Component of a Curriculum of Connections Unit

Session Overview

In this workshop, participants will create appropriate and effective introductory activities for a Curriculum of Connections unit.

Masters

- Designing Introductory Activities in the Curriculum of Connections
- Sample Introductory Activities for a Curriculum of Connections Unit

Session Details

Introduction

- If necessary, review the definition and characteristics of introductory activities (Workshop #6). Ask participants how they might expect introductory activities in a Connections unit to differ from those in a Core unit.
- Distribute "Designing Introductory Activities in the Curriculum of Connections." Choose a suggestion from the handout at random and ask how or why that would "fit" the Curriculum of Connections. Ask for evidence that the activity also reflects the Core Curriculum, since that curriculum remains at the heart of all the parallels.
- The hefty list of suggestions on the handout should get participants thinking about new options for introductory activities or those they have done in the past and could adapt for use in this parallel. Invite them to scan the list of suggestions and share their own experiences in leading or participating in similar activities. Suggest that they highlight one or two ideas that seem interesting and/or new to them. Challenge them to incorporate these activities in their unit.

Teaching and Learning Activities

- Share "Sample Introductory Activities for a Curriculum of Connections Unit." Discuss ways in which these activities serve the purposes of the Curriculum of Connections, as well as the Core Curriculum.
- Instruct participants to work in small groups (or individually) to create or redesign introductory activities so that they are in alignment with the Curriculum of Connections.

Closure/Looking Forward

Allow time for groups to share specific examples with one another and provide feedback. Encourage them to highlight how their work incorporates the unique qualities of the Curriculum of Connections (see "Checklist for Designing Curriculum Within the Curriculum of Connections Parallel") and/or provides opportunities to address the driving questions of that parallel (see "Driving Questions of the Curriculum of Connections" in Appendix D).

DESIGNING INTRODUCTORY ACTIVITIES IN THE CURRICULUM OF CONNECTIONS

- Provide students with concept maps.
- Develop and share advance organizers that list the major concepts, principles, skills, and dispositions they will acquire in this unit.
- Introduce the ideas of macroconcepts, generalizations, and themes. Contrast these terms with concepts, rules, and principles.
- Share a familiar Aesop's fable with students or ask them to identify and list common axioms, adages, or proverbs. Ask students to discuss and identify the purpose for proverbs and axioms. Explain that this unit of instruction will have a similar purpose.
- Provide students with three parts of an analogy or a portion of a simile. Ask them to complete the missing portions. Discuss why or how they use analogies or similes in their daily lives.
- Make a list of the many ways that analogies, metaphors, and similes support new learning, decrease confusion, or enhance problem solving. Explain that the purpose of this unit will be to build the same kinds of bridges and connections for students.
- Develop and share focusing questions that bridge two or more concepts, skills, principles, or dispositions and these multidisciplinary themes and macroconcepts.
- Prepare a list of the concepts, skills, principles, and dispositions students will learn during this unit. Next to each, print a symbol or a bridge, connection, umbrella, and so on. Tell students that throughout the integrated unit they will continually search for the words or terms they can use to describe the macroconcepts, dispositions, processes, generalizations, or themes that apply to similar classes or relations across multiple disciplines or topics.
- Introduce an intriguing problem or puzzle in a topic or discipline distant from the unit or discipline students are about to begin studying. Tell students that careful reflection during the course of this unit should help them discover macroconcepts, themes, generalization, or analogies that will, in turn, help them solve the cross-discipline puzzle or problem by the end of the unit.

Adapted from *The Parallel Curriculum* (Tomlinson, et al., 2008) Figure 5.3.

SAMPLE INTRODUCTORY ACTIVITIES FOR A CURRICULUM OF CONNECTIONS UNIT

Example 1: Flight Unit

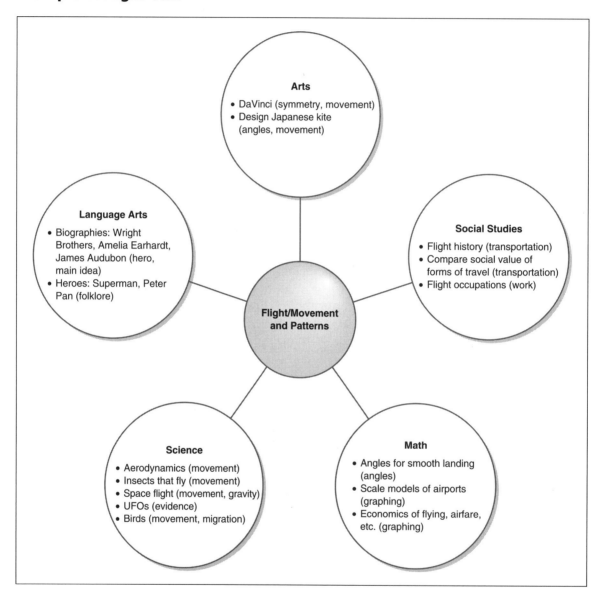

Example 2: American Revolution Simulation

The purpose of this simulation is to allow students to connect with the feelings and emotions colonists felt under Britain's rule. At the end of the simulation, students will identify with the colonists' sense of Britain's injustice and their decision to go to war. This simulation is conducted at the start of a unit on the American Revolution.

Activity Details

Part 1: Proposal and Responses

1. Students read "Suggested Revision to Current Calendar" (provided) in groups. You can revise it to apply more specifically to your school site, or you can merely use it as it is written.

2. After reading, instruct students to take out one sheet of paper per group and title it "Student Response to Calendar Revision." On this sheet, they are to provide a list of their reactions. If they list grievances, ask them to provide support for each grievance. Students make one list per group.

3. Invite your principal (or vice principal) into your class to say something like the following to your students:

> "You have just read a proposal by our superintendent. In it, she makes a strong argument for extending the school day and the school year so that our students can become competitive with other students around the world. Many schools in other places have lengthened their school days already and have implemented a year-round school schedule.
>
> "I want you all to take a look at this plan and respond to it prior to the upcoming board meeting. I thought that by hearing from students, the superintendent might revise her plan, since she believes student voice is important in decision making. I'm not sure she'll really look at what you've written or make any changes based on what you've said, but it's worth a try. Please write neatly on the sheet ('Student Response to Calendar Revision') so the superintendent can easily read it. Then, turn it in to your teacher. Thank you."

4. Once the response sheets are filled out, have one person from each group read the group's list to the class. Collect these lists to use during the "Debriefing."

Part 2: Debriefing

1. Later in the day or at the next class meeting, have students reconvene in groups and provide the rationale for presenting the proposal. Make sure that you conduct this debriefing before the end of the day so students do not go home and share with parents that the district is actually revising the calendar! Your script might go something like this:

> "This morning you had a chance to look at a recent proposal. Here are some of your reactions (read some of the strong group responses that were shared earlier). It seems that there is an overwhelming disdain for this revised schedule.
>
> "Our next unit deals with the Revolutionary War—or the American Revolution, as some call it. Much of what you are feeling toward the superintendent and her proposal is what the American colonists felt toward King George, parliament, and their policies. Even though parliament had a lot to do with the policies, King George was the target of their anger.
>
> "American colonists did not have a say in government and the policies set forth. They were being taxed like crazy and did not see the benefits. England was in debt from the French and Indian War and expected the colonists to pay its debt. So, King George and parliament created different acts or laws (e.g., Tea Act, Stamp Act, Intolerable Acts) designed to tax the people. The taxes the colonists paid went toward the war debt.
>
> "So that angry parents and students do not barrage the superintendent with calls, the truth is that the proposal you read about a revised calendar was a fake. It was an activity designed to rile you so you had a taste of what the American colonists felt. In this next unit, you'll have a chance to learn specifically about the different actions of England that angered the colonists.

"Now let's investigate the causes of war. Name some wars in history besides the Revolutionary War (e.g., Civil War, World War I, World War II, Korean War, Desert Storm). In your groups, you are to choose a recorder who will record any causes of war your group members' feel contributed to *any* war. You can record your answers on the sheet titled 'Causes of the Revolution.'"

2. Have students take out one sheet of paper per group and title it "Causes of War" and brainstorm possible causes of any war. Remind them to make a list using numbers or bullets and not paragraphs. This will help teach a miniskill of creating a list. When they are finished, conduct a discussion in which each group shares and responds to causes of war.

SUGGESTED REVISION TO CURRENT CALENDAR

Currently, students in our school district attend school about 180 days, which include Parent Conference Days. Teachers are contracted to come approximately 184 days; hence, the extra four days teachers attend school and students do not.

In most other developed countries, such as Japan, Germany, and England, students attend school significantly more than American children do. In these countries, year-round school is not uncommon. Some administrators in school districts in the U.S. have realized that year-round schools would be beneficial to students and have thus adopted a year-round calendar for their students. Many maintain that providing year-round schooling and lengthening the school day will keep students off the streets, improve student learning, and help to provide American children with the knowledge they need to compete in the world at large. After reviewing much research, I am proposing the following for our school district. This plan is expected to be approved by the School Board and go into effect in one month:

Extend the school day by one hour and ten minutes.

Saturday School will be implemented. Those students who arrive tardy to two classes or to school within a given two-week period will be required to attend two consecutive days at Saturday School. Tardy is defined as any student not in his or her seat at the time the bell rings for class to begin. Teachers may deem it necessary to give Saturday School detention if the need arises for other situations, as well (e.g., constant reminders of taking off hats or chewing gum, inappropriate conduct).

Recess will be eliminated each Friday to allow for an all-school reading time. Each Friday during recess, students will remain silent throughout the entire school and read their independent reading books. Students who fail to remain silent or who consistently forget to bring a book will attend three consecutive days at Saturday School.

A year-round school will replace the nine-month school year. All students will attend school throughout the year with the exception of one three-week break.

When students have satisfied certain requirements in each subject area (e.g., Math, Language Arts, Science), they will pass to the next grade. Tests will be given in **each** subject area to determine if students will move to the next grade level. Some students will automatically remain at a current grade level until **all** subject area tests are passed.

Hopefully, the aforementioned changes will provide a greater learning opportunity for our students so they will be better prepared to face the challenges of middle school, high school, and beyond.

WORKSHOP #19

Teaching Strategies Component of a Curriculum of Connections Unit

Session Overview

In this workshop, participants will identify appropriate teaching strategies for a Curriculum of Connections unit.

Masters

- Teaching Strategies for the Curriculum of Connections Parallel

Session Details

Introduction

- If necessary, review the definition and characteristics of teaching strategies (Workshop #7). Ask participants to suggest teaching strategies that might be particularly useful and not so useful in a Curriculum of Connections unit and to explain their thinking.
- Share "Teaching Strategies for the Curriculum of Connections Parallel" and compare these suggestions to the results of the earlier discussion. Choose a strategy at random.

Ask: "How does this strategy specifically promote the goals of the Curriculum of Connections? Of the Core Curriculum?"

Teaching and Learning Activities

Say: "Although both the Core Curriculum and the Curriculum of Connections incorporate varied pedagogy, coaching, and scaffolding, the pedagogies used most often in the Curriculum of Connections promote students' ability to perceive, understand, and appreciate the connections across topics, disciplines, and concepts. Within this parallel, the teacher often serves as a mediator between student and new learning, building bridges that enable students to perceive or demonstrate a connection between two different sets of information, two or more concepts, or two or more principles."

Continue to encourage participants to work in teams. Allow them time to identify appropriate teaching methods that are in alignment with the Curriculum of Connections Parallel for their targeted lessons or unit. Encourage them to try to incorporate a new-to-them teaching strategy into their unit.

Closure/Looking Forward

Encourage each group to share one or more of the teaching methods they selected for a particular Curriculum of Connections lesson or unit of study and talk about what the strategy would look like in their classroom. As groups share, record the strategies they have chosen. Ask the group to examine the shared list to see if there is a consistent thread of methods selected. Ask why they think these strategies were chosen most often. Highlight or ask them to highlight how the strategies they plan to use support the unique qualities of the Curriculum of Connections, as well as remain true to the intents and purposes of the Core Curriculum. (See "Checklist for Designing Curriculum Within the Curriculum of Connections Parallel" and/or "Driving Questions of the Curriculum of Connections" in Appendix D.)

TEACHING STRATEGIES FOR THE CURRICULUM OF CONNECTIONS PARALLEL

- Use the synectics teaching model to help students build a bridge between the concepts, principles, and dispositions in one unit and analogous concepts, principles, skills, and dispositions in another model.
- Share or help students create metaphors to build bridges between topics and disciplines.
- Use Socratic questioning and deductive logic as scaffolds to help students make connections between abstract units, classes, and relations, and systems.
- Provide opportunities for students to work in cooperative groups as they make analogies between topics, events, and disciplines.
- Use examples and nonexamples within the Concept Attainment Model to help students develop macroconcepts and themes.
- Improvise on Wasserman's (1988) Play-Debrief-Replay teaching methods. Help students acquire and reflect on learned concepts and principles, and then replay the use of the same concepts and principles with another venue. Follow with another debriefing and reflection opportunity.
- Use intradisciplinary or interdisciplinary problem-solving simulations or scenarios to support the development of macroconcepts.

Adapted from *The Parallel Curriculum* (Tomlinson, et al., 2008) Figure 5.3.

WORKSHOP #20

Learning Activities Component of a Curriculum of Connections Unit

Session Overview

In this workshop, participants will design or remodel learning activities to meet the intents and purposes of the Curriculum of Connections.

Masters

- Learning Activity Suggestions for the Curriculum of Connections Parallel
- Comparing Cinderellas

Session Details

Introduction

- If necessary, revisit the definition and characteristics of learning activities (Workshop #8). Distribute a selection of learning activities that participants constructed for their Core Curriculum unit, or have participants recall and briefly share a learning activity they crafted. Ask participants to suggest ways to recraft the activities to highlight the intents and purposes of the Curriculum of Connections.
- Share "Learning Activity Suggestions for the Curriculum of Connections Parallel" and compare these suggestions to the results of the earlier discussion.

Teaching and Learning Activities

- Share the "Comparing Cinderellas" activity from an elementary classroom. Note that the same kind of activity could be used in a secondary classroom just by changing the literature involved. Discuss ways in which the teacher infused the intents and purposes of the Curriculum of Connections and Core Curriculum parallels. Solicit other ways the teacher might highlight these intents and purposes.
- Have participants create appropriate Curriculum of Connections learning activities. Suggest they refer to the "Driving Questions of the Curriculum of Connections" to help stimulate their thinking.

Closure/Looking Forward

Allow time for groups to share specific examples with one another and provide feedback. Encourage them to highlight how their work incorporates the unique qualities of the Curriculum of Connections (see "Checklist for Designing Curriculum Within the Curriculum of Connections Parallel") and/or provides opportunities to address the driving questions of that parallel (see "Driving Questions of the Curriculum of Connections" in Appendix D).

LEARNING ACTIVITY SUGGESTIONS FOR THE CURRICULUM OF CONNECTIONS PARALLEL

Develop learning activities related to content acquisition that require students to identify connections, acquire macroconcepts, make cross-discipline generalizations, and use themes to solve integrated problems. Involve students in the use of the following thinking skills.

- Comparing and contrasting
- Deductive and inductive thinking
- Making analogies
- Creative problem solving
- Making generalizations
- Hierarchical classification
- Seeing patterns and relationships
- Developing insights
- Systems thinking

COMPARING CINDERELLAS

Goal:

Compare and contrast different versions of Cinderella from various cultures.

Resources:

- Various versions of the Cinderella tale (or versions of another popular fairy tale)
- Venn diagram or a similar organizational chart

Lesson Details:

1. Focus on many versions of the favorite fairy tale *Cinderella.* Begin by reading the European version by Charles Perrault, which is the most familiar tale.

2. Then read other versions from different countries, plus some modern and humorous ones, such as:

- *Yeh-Shen* (China)
- *Mufaro's Beautiful Daughters* (Africa)
- *The Rough-Face Girl* (Native America)
- *The Egyptian Cinderella*
- *Prince Cinders*
- *Dinorella*
- *Cinderella Penguin*
- *Cinder Elly*
- *Cinderella Bigfoot*

3. Lead a discussion with students in which you compare and contrast these various stories. Then, have students use a Venn diagram or other organizational structure to record the similarities and differences. Discuss with students what they recorded on their Venn diagrams or charts paying particular attention to the connection among these stories.

4. Focus on the big ideas of the unit through these guiding questions: How do characters in these stories act in similar ways? How are the themes in these fairy tales similar? How do these themes connect with other stories? Other genres?

WORKSHOP #21

Grouping Practices Component of a Curriculum of Connections Unit

Session Overview

In this workshop, participants will assign grouping practices to their learning activities so that the grouping practices enhance the intents and purposes of this parallel.

Masters

- Grouping Suggestions for the Curriculum of Connections

Session Details

Introduction
- If necessary, revisit the definition and characteristics of grouping practices (Workshop #9). Ask participants to talk about ways in which various grouping practices might be used to support the intents and purposes of the Curriculum of Connections.
- Distribute "Grouping Suggestions for the Curriculum of Connections."

Then say: "While all kinds of grouping practices find a place in a Curriculum of Connections unit, small groups and dyads are particularly useful as they allow students to work collaboratively, provide constructive feedback to each other, and participate in the critical, deductive, and inductive thinking so closely associated with the Curriculum of Connections. Students need opportunities to make hypotheses, argue the merits of their conclusions, listen to others' perspectives, and refine their own thinking. In a well-constructed Curriculum of Connections, the room is a busy place, filled with students engaged in speculation, debate, and a search for corroboration evidence."

Teaching and Learning Activities

- Because group work is so integral to this parallel, spend time sharing strategies or methods for helping students learn to work well in groups, such as organizing materials, assigning responsibilities, assessing group work, and so on.
- In small groups or individually, as appropriate, have participants review the work they have created thus far with attention to the kinds of grouping configurations they may wish to employ. Encourage them to incorporate a variety of grouping strategies into their unit design. Some participants may find it useful to take an activity they have designed for one type of grouping and refashion it to fit another type of grouping, noting how the type of grouping impacts student learning.

Closure/Looking Forward

Ask participants to critique each others' work thus far in the unit, looking for variety of grouping strategies over time and evaluating the degree to which their grouping choices support the unique qualities of the Curriculum of Connections (see "Checklist for Designing Curriculum Within the Curriculum of Connections Parallel") and/or provide students with opportunities to address the driving questions of that parallel (see "Driving Questions of the Curriculum of Connections" in Appendix D).

GROUPING SUGGESTIONS FOR THE CURRICULUM OF CONNECTIONS

- Work with large groups of students to present the goals of the unit, provide directions, and share information about macroconcepts, generalizations, and processes.
- Use pairs and small groups of students to support pattern finding and the development of macroconcepts and themes.
- Briefly conference with individual students to assess the degree to which they can relate interdisciplinary examples and real-world problems to core concepts and principles.
- Observe individual students and provide feedback to support the development of cognitive skills.
- Debrief students in large groups, using maps and diagrams, to ensure that the entire class can connect macroconcepts, generalizations, and processes to core concepts and principles.

Adapted from *The Parallel Curriculum* (Tomlinson, et al., 2008) Figure 5.3.

WORKSHOP #22

Resources Component of a Curriculum of Connections Unit

Session Overview

In this workshop, participants will identify student and teacher resources that would help them design and carry out a Curriculum of Connections unit.

Masters

- Resources Suggestions for the Curriculum of Connections Parallel

Session Details

Introduction

- Now that teachers are deep in the process of remodeling lessons to be in alignment with the Curriculum of Connections Parallel, they most likely have given some thought to the student and teacher resources they will use. Revisit the sheet "Resources" (Workshop #9) if you feel participants need to be reminded of the definition and characteristics of this key component.
- Remind participants that in the "Comparing Cinderellas" activity in the previous workshop, the teacher had sought out a variety of versions of that story. Tell participants that, in this parallel, lessons commonly include content and make use of resources from more than one author, event, culture, topic, or discipline.

Teaching and Learning Activities

- Ask participants to list the characteristics of resources that would be particularly helpful in designing and teaching a Curriculum of Connections unit. Share "Resources Suggestions for the Curriculum of Connections Parallel" to affirm and extend their thinking.
- Acknowledge that finding the time to locate a variety of resources is challenging. Encourage them to share resources with one another and commit to adding to their resource library over time. If participants are not familiar with the unit topics their colleagues are pursuing for their unit design, take time to share the topics now and encourage them to all be on the lookout for resources that may be helpful to them and their colleagues.
- Give teachers the opportunity to reflect on their work thus far and to identify resources that would help them ensure that their unit reflects the intents and purposes of the Curriculum of Connections. Suggest that the driving questions of this parallel may help them in their work.

Closure/Looking Forward

Allow time for groups to share specific resource ideas and how they would make use of them. As always, encourage them to highlight how the resources they choose incorporate the unique qualities of the Curriculum of Connections (see "Checklist for Designing Curriculum Within the Curriculum of Connections Parallel") and/or provide opportunities to address the driving questions of that parallel (see "Driving Questions of the Curriculum of Connections" in Appendix D).

RESOURCES SUGGESTIONS FOR THE CURRICULUM OF CONNECTIONS PARALLEL

- Provide students with concept maps and advance organizers that preview the important concepts and principles explored in the unit.
- Find high school texts and college resources to identify the major concepts, skills, and principles within related fields and disciplines.
- Provide graphic organizers to support analogy making, creative problem solving, and classification.
- Identify and locate numerous interdisciplinary examples related to the concepts, principles, skills, and dispositions being addressed in the unit.
- Find photographs, journals, data, primary source documents, newspaper articles, historical accounts, magazine articles, Web sites, paintings, and so on that address the same concept or illustrate the same principles in various disciplines.
- Locate an interdisciplinary problem or simulation related to the unit's learning goals.
- Provide biographies of historical and contemporary inquires, inventors, and researchers in various disciplines who used the same concepts or processes.

Adapted from *The Parallel Curriculum* (Tomlinson, et al., 2008) Figure 5.3.

WORKSHOP #23

Products Component of a Curriculum of Connections Unit

Session Overview

In this workshop, participants will remodel or design unit products to match the intents and purposes of the Curriculum of Connections Parallel.

Masters

- Product Suggestions for the Curriculum of Connections Parallel
- Student Assignment

Session Details

Introduction

- If necessary, revisit the definition and characteristics of products (Workshop #11).

Say: "The difference between product assignments in a Core Curriculum unit and a Curriculum of Connections unit is that the Core Curriculum would call on students to identify, apply, and illustrate frameworks of meaning and skill within a particular discipline, whereas the latter calls on students to deal with those frameworks across disciplines, topics, periods, cultures, and so on."

- Distribute and discuss "Product Suggestions for the Curriculum of Connections Parallel."

(Continued)

(Continued)

Ask: "What products have you assigned that might be altered successfully to be in alignment with a Curriculum of Connections unit?"

- Refer to the product list on "Products" (Workshop #11).

Ask: "Which of these products might be a natural fit for the Curriculum of Connections?" Why do you say so?

Teaching and Learning Activities

- Distribute "Student Assignment." Explain that this is a product designed while teaching the causes of the American Revolution. In this assignment, students connect with the colonists by also declaring their independence. It guides them to look at the driving questions of the Curriculum of Connections. A teacher could easily adapt this assignment within this parallel by asking students to write from the perspective of another group and/or to a different audience still using the format of the Declaration of Independence. For example, students could assume the role of black South Africans during apartheid and write the document from this point of view to the government of South Africa declaring their independence from the system of apartheid that binds them.
- Remind participants that product assignment in the Curriculum of Connection should cause students to consider the following.
  - o How do the ideas I have learned work in other contexts? (In this case, their own lives.)
  - o How does looking at one thing help me understand another?
  - o In what ways is it beneficial for me to examine varied perspectives on a problem or issue? (As they declare their independence, help them to examine the perspectives of a potential recipient of their document.)
  - o What connections do I see between what I am studying and my own life and times?
- Ask participants to create or refashion a product assignment for their unit that reinforces the intents and purposes of the Curriculum of Connections Parallel as it focuses on key unit concepts and principles.

Closure/Looking Forward

Ask participants to exchange product assignments. They should consider:
- Is the product worthy of study and teacher time?
- To what extent does it focus on unit concepts and principles?
- To what degree is the product in alignment with the intents and purposes of the Curriculum of Connections and the Core Curriculum?
- What are some ways this link might be strengthened?
- What other product assignments might allow the student to accomplish similar goals *and* help students make other important or interesting connections?

PRODUCT SUGGESTIONS FOR THE CURRICULUM OF CONNECTIONS PARALLEL

- Ask students to create graphic displays that explain the patterns they have identified across topics, events, people, or disciplines.
- Create an imaginary forum, similar to Steve Allen's old television show *Meeting of the Minds,* in which students take on the role of various historical figures across time as they discuss a contemporary or historical problem or issue (Bourman, 1996).
- Assign concept maps to analyze the acquisition of macroconcepts and integrated principles.

- Ask students to demonstrate the relationship between the core concepts and principles in one topic, discipline, or event, to those in another field or period.
- Ask students to demonstrate their knowledge of integrated connections through the use of reflective essays, journal entries, charts, diagrams, analogies, and collages.
- Provide graphic organizers or double-entry journals that enable students to communicate their acquisition of macroconcepts and generalizations.
- Ask students to create a synectics diagram to demonstrate the use of metaphoric thinking to solve an interdisciplinary problem.

Adapted from *The Parallel Curriculum* (Tomlinson, et al., 2008) Figure 5.3.

STUDENT ASSIGNMENT

Declaration of Independence/U.S. History

DUE DATE:_____ **PAGE LENGTH:**
At least one page and a half

We have been studying the format and content of the Declaration of Independence. Your job is to use the format to create a situation in which *you* declare your independence from something, someone, or a group. This can be an actual situation or one that you invent. Write a declaration of independence for this situation that includes the listed parts below. As you write this, please begin each part with the titles used below (Part I, Part II, Part III, Part IV). Do not forget to include a title.

PART I
Introduction that simply states from what you are declaring your independence.

PART II
State your beliefs about the issue. For instance, in the U.S. Declaration of Independence, some colonists' beliefs were:

- All men were created equal.
- God has given all men some basic rights, and these cannot be taken from them.
- Government should not be changed for small or unimportant reasons.

Include at least four beliefs about your issue.

PART III
Explain what wrongs you feel have been done that have resulted in you declaring your independence. For instance, in the Declaration of Independence, some chief wrongs included:

- The king did not let the colonists make all the laws they needed for their own good.
- The king taxed the colonists without letting them vote in parliament on the taxes.
- The king would not let colonists trade with other countries.

Include at least four wrongs.

PART IV

Finally, *explain what decisions you have made to declare your independence* from whatever or whomever. For instance, in the Declaration of Independence, the decisions included:

- "We say that these states are no longer under the rule of England and its king."
- "We, the representatives of the United States of America, by the power given to us by the people in these colonies, say that these united colonies are, and have the right to be, free and independent states."

WORKSHOP #24

Extension Activities Component of a Curriculum of Connections Unit

Session Overview

In this workshop, participants will design or remodel extension activities to match the intents and purposes of the Curriculum of Connections Parallel.

Masters

- Extension Activity Suggestions for the Curriculum of Connections

Session Details

Introduction

- If necessary, revisit the definition and characteristics of extension activities (Workshop #12).

Say: "Because of the interrelatedness of knowledge, it is useful for a teacher to help students explore key macroconcepts and generalizations in areas of particular interest to students. In this regard, extension activities are a natural for the Curriculum of Connections."

- Ask participants to discuss how they might recognize a student in need of an extension activity. Discuss the importance of incorporating student interests into the design of an extension activity and how the Curriculum of Connections might help students *expand* their interests.

Teaching and Learning Activities

- Share "Extension Activity Suggestions for the Curriculum of Connections."
- Instruct participants to work alone or in groups to create extension activities for the lessons or units they are redesigning. Suggest they have specific students in mind as they design possible extensions.

Closure/Looking Forward

Ask volunteers to share their work and describe a specific student or type of student that would find the extension intriguing and satisfying. Be sure they also share or solicit comments on the degree to which their extension incorporates the unique qualities of the Curriculum of Connections (see "Checklist for Designing Curriculum Within the Curriculum of Connections Parallel") and/or provides opportunities to address the driving questions of that parallel (see "Driving Questions of the Curriculum of Connections" in Appendix D).

EXTENSION ACTIVITY SUGGESTIONS FOR THE CURRICULUM OF CONNECTIONS

- Team with another content area specialist and identify macroconcepts, themes, dispositions, and interdisciplinary processes that can be incorporated concurrently or within two or more consecutively taught units of instruction. Design related learning centers, independent projects, problem-solving activities, and so on.
- Ask content area specialists and other teachers who are experts in the concepts, principles, dispositions, and processes within one field or discipline to coplan, team teach, coach, or provide useful feedback on the progress and success of the extension activities.
- Ask resource specialists to provide Connections extensions to interested students during resource or pull-out time.
- Provide interested students with an opportunity to study philosophy, wisdom, and epistemology.
- Teach students the process of hierarchical classification or systems thinking.
- Teach students how to use the synectics model for making analogies or for problem solving.
- Develop a simulated or real-world problem that students can solve by applying the concepts, principles, skills, and dispositions of one field to another topic or discipline.
- Provide opportunities for students to interview and visit with artists, researchers, college professors, philosophers, and interdisciplinary problem-solving teams to discuss how they use knowledge in other fields and disciplines in their daily work and problem solving.

Adapted from *The Parallel Curriculum* (Tomlinson, et al., 2008) Figure 5.3.

WORKSHOP #25

Differentiation and AID Component of a Curriculum of Connections Unit

Note to Facilitator

To prepare for this workshop, you may wish to review Chapter 8, "Ascending Intellectual Demand in the Parallel Curriculum Model," of *The Parallel Curriculum* (Tomlinson, et al., 2008).

Session Overview

In this workshop, participants will design appropriate differentiation and Ascending Intellectual Demand (AID) opportunities that match the intents and purposes of this parallel.

Masters

- Suggestions for Differentiation and AID in the Curriculum of Connections Parallel
- AID and the Curriculum of Connections Parallel

(Continued)

(Continued)

Session Details

Introduction

- If necessary, revisit "Differentiation Based on Learner Need" and "Ascending Intellectual Demand" from Workshop #13.
- Ask participants to share their experiences with differentiation and AID in their Core Curriculum units. Focus on the degree to which they felt the differentiated activities matched student needs, how they matched students to differentiated tasks, and any management or assessments issues that arose.

Teaching and Learning Activities

Say: "All students should work with connections-making curriculum. As students continue to develop throughout a unit of study, effective teachers provide appropriate differentiation to match varied learner needs in terms of readiness, interest, and learning preferences."

- Distribute "Suggestions for Differentiation and AID in the Curriculum of Connections Parallel" and discuss ways in which these suggestions focus on making connections, yet allow for student differences in this skill.

Say: "Ascending Intellectual Demand, you will remember, is a specific type of differentiation designed to help students develop along a continuum of expertise in a discipline. In the Curriculum of Connections, AID also will help students develop expertise in making both inter- and intradisciplinary connections."

- Distribute "AID and the Curriculum of Connections Parallel." Discuss ways in which the suggested modifications push students toward greater expertise.
- Ask participants to chose one or more components of their unit and differentiate for learner variance and/or ascending intellectual demand. Remind them to be ready to show how their differentiation and/or AID enhances the student's learning **and** remains faithful to the intent and purposes of this parallel.

Closure/Looking Forward

Ask volunteers to share their work. In doing so, they should describe a specific student or type of student for whom their differentiation or AID is designed. Be sure they also share or solicit comments from their colleagues on the degree to which their work incorporates the unique qualities of the Curriculum of Connections (see "Checklist for Designing Curriculum Within the Curriculum of Connections Parallel") and/or provides opportunities to address the driving questions of that parallel (see "Driving Questions of the Curriculum of Connections" in Appendix D).

SUGGESTIONS FOR DIFFERENTIATION AND AID IN THE CURRICULUM OF CONNECTIONS PARALLEL

- Increase or decrease teacher scaffolding to support the development of macroconcepts, interdisciplinary processes and dispositions, themes, and systems thinking.
- Provide additional representative topics for comparison to reduce ambiguity or to add additional layers of complexity. Keep these topics within the same discipline

to decrease cognitive difficulty or expand to other disciplines to increase intellectual demand.
- Use less obvious topics or disciplines for comparison with students with more sophisticated levels of deductive thinking. Encourage a continuing commitment to intrinsic motivation and to the world of ideas.
- Use the parallel's guidelines for Ascending Intellectual Demand in selecting resources and designing learning activities and products.

Adapted from *The Parallel Curriculum* (Tomlinson, et al., 2008) Figure 5.3.

AID AND THE CURRICULUM OF CONNECTIONS PARALLEL

To promote Ascending Intellectual Demand:

- Increase the unfamiliarity of the context or problem in which understandings or skills are applied.
- Ask students to generate defensible criteria against which they then weigh diverse perspectives on a problem or solution (or use professional criteria for the same purpose).
- Call on students to develop solutions, proposals, or approaches that effectively bridge differences in perspective but still effectively address the problem.
- Ask students to make proposals or predictions for future directions based on student-generated, discipline-related patterns from the past in a particular domain.
- Have students search for legitimate and useful connections among seemingly disparate elements (e.g., music and medicine or law and geography).
- Develop tasks or products that seek patterns of interaction among multiple areas (e.g., ways in which geography, economics, politics, and technology affect one another).
- Call on students to look at broad swaths of the world through a perspective quite unlike their own (e.g., how an age mate from a culture and economy very different from the student's would react to the student's house, slang, religion, clothing, music, relationships with adults, toys or gadgets, plans for the future, and so on).
- Develop tasks and products that seek out unstated assumptions beneath the surface of beliefs, decisions, approaches, or perspectives.
- Ask students to develop systems for making connections, drawing generalizations, achieving balanced perspectives, or addressing problems.
- Design criteria for students' work that call for a higher standard of quality (such as insightful, highly illustrative, highly synthetic, unusually articulate or expressive, and so on) as opposed to a less demanding but still positive standard of quality (such as appropriate, accurate, feasible, informed, defensible, and so on).

Adapted from *The Parallel Curriculum* (Tomlinson, et al., 2008) Figure 5.10.

Some Specific Examples

Lesson Background	AID Example
In a cultural adaptation unit for elementary students, teachers provide information about a culture students are studying currently or have studied previously to prove that "Adaptation is necessary for survival." Students respond to several statements about culture based on information learned thus far, for example: • "All cultures rise and fall." • "The rigidity of a culture could lead to its demise or end."	The introduction of additional big ideas in the context of the lesson provides the opportunity to stimulate more depth and complexity of understanding. This is one method for achieving AID. Advanced students should begin to realize that big ideas interact. Encourage these students to compare and contrast the ways targeted cultural groups in various time segments adapted as a means of survival.
In a middle or high school unit on exponents, students work on a discovery activity to find common characteristics of exponential functions.	Students who can easily complete the family of functions activity should be urged to explore other exponential functions. They should test different possibilities and try to come up with more characteristics. Some possibilities include putting a negative or a number in front of the a^x term.
During one comparative analysis lesson in a high school unit on biography and autobiography in which students understand challenge, choice, and chance, students look for recurring patterns of behavior, environmental and personality traits, skills, dispositions, and products of individuals. They then label these characteristics so that commonalities can be detected.	During the final analysis, ask students who need more challenge to identify if and how the perspectives of these individuals were shaped by time, place, cultures, events, and circumstances.

WORKSHOP #26

Closure Component of a Curriculum of Connections Unit

Session Overview

In this workshop, participants will design closure activities for their unit that match the intents and purposes of the Curriculum of Connections Parallel.

Masters

• Suggestions for Closure in the Curriculum of Connections Parallel

Session Details

Introduction

• If necessary, revisit the definition and characteristics of closure (Workshop #14).
• Ask participants to share their experiences with closure activities in their Core Curriculum unit. What went well? What might they have done differently?

Teaching and Learning Activities

- Distribute and discuss "Suggestions for Closure in the Curriculum of Connections Parallel."
- Ask participants to design an appropriate closure activity for their unit. Remind them that as in a Core Curriculum unit, it is important that closure activities focus on the meaning of the unit and its associated activities, but also remind students of the interconnectedness of knowledge.

Closure/Looking Forward

Ask participants to critique each others' work, evaluating the degree to which their closure activities incorporate the unique qualities of the Curriculum of Connections (see "Checklist for Designing Curriculum Within the Curriculum of Connections Parallel") and/or provide opportunities to address the driving questions of that parallel (see "Driving Questions of the Curriculum of Connections" in Appendix D).

SUGGESTIONS FOR CLOSURE IN THE CURRICULUM OF CONNECTIONS PARALLEL

- Guide students in reflecting on key concepts and closure principles in one segment of study that can help them achieve understanding in another segment of study.
- Ask students to make connections between what they are studying and their own experiences.
- Have students propose examples from music, arts, sports, technology, or other interests that seem to operate according to the concepts and principles they are studying in class.
- Guide students in thinking about differences in the way particular concepts are used in one context versus another, or ways in which principles might be reworded slightly to reflect a particular context.
- Spotlight key information, vocabulary, and skills from the lesson or unit.
- Ask and explore answers to the driving questions of the Curriculum of Connections.

Adapted from *The Parallel Curriculum* (Tomlinson, et al., 2008) Figure 5.3.

Note to Facilitator

As you progress through subsequent sessions, continue to lead participants through each key component as you did in the previous two parallels. Like before, you will introduce and discuss a curriculum component and provide suggestions on how to make that component take on the flavor of Parallel of Practice. After each component is featured, allow time for participants to remodel or create lessons so they are in alignment with the Curriculum of Practice. The format of this guide, however, will vary from earlier chapters. For those sessions devoted to a curriculum component you have only been provided with "Session Objectives" and a list of "Masters." Continue to use solid teaching methodologies as you work with participants (see Appendix A). Keep in mind that by this point in the series of workshops, some may move faster than others through the components. Others will prefer to look at their unit design in a more holistic fashion. Don't feel absolutely tied to following the sequence of components as presented. There may be participants who just want to be given the set of handouts for this parallel and go on from there.

The Curriculum of Practice

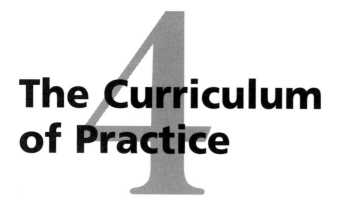

Note to Facilitator

To prepare for the workshops in this chapter, you may wish to review Chapter 6, "The Curriculum of Practice Parallel" in *The Parallel Curriculum* by Tomlinson, et al. (2008).

WORKSHOP #27

The Curriculum of Practice Parallel

Session Objectives

This session focuses on the basic tenets of the Curriculum of Practice, specifically its definition, intent, benefits, and driving questions.

Masters

- Nuts and Bolts of the Curriculum of Practice Parallel
- Curriculum of Practice at Work in the Classroom
- Checklist for Designing Curriculum Within the Curriculum of Practice Parallel

Session Details

Introduction

- First, review with participants that there are four ways of approaching curriculum. Reintroduce the "The Parallel Curriculum" (Workshop #1) and draw attention to the third parallel—the *Curriculum of Practice*.
- Ask participants what they think of when they hear the word *practitioner*. (They may immediately mention *doctor*.) Lead them to a discussion about what a practitioner of a discipline would do. Help them realize that a practitioner can be either a practicing member of a particular profession or occupation, or a scholar of that discipline.

- Ask participants if this type of curriculum is familiar to them. Ask them to share their experiences.
- Explain that the focus for this next series of workshops is to help them understand the purpose, intent, and driving questions associated with this parallel and then directly apply what they learn to remodeling a chosen lesson(s) or unit to be in alignment with this parallel.

Teaching and Learning Activities

Say: "The purpose of the Curriculum of Practice is to help students function with increasing skill and confidence as professionals in a discipline would function. This parallel is devoted to the promotion of expertise as a practitioner or scholar of the discipline. As you know, the Core Curriculum begins with students acquiring knowledge of the key facts, concepts, and principles within a discipline. The Curriculum of Practice extends these understandings by enabling students to "practice" or to learn firsthand how to use the skills and methodologies used by practicing professionals in various disciplines to answer their questions, to prove the meaning of the key ideas of the discipline, and to test their adaptability with those ideas. While the Core Curriculum and the Curriculum of Practice are related, the key difference between them is that the Curriculum of Practice places in the foreground of consideration the methods and skills used by practicing experts or scholars in a discipline."

- Distribute and discuss "Nuts and Bolts of the Curriculum of Practice Parallel."

Ask: "Why should we design curriculum that offers students opportunities to work as a practitioners and/or scholars? What's in it for them? What's in it for us? In what ways has this series of workshops allowed us to engage in Curriculum of Practice-like work?"

- Distribute "Curriculum of Practice at Work in the Classroom." This gives a brief overview of what two teachers did within a Curriculum of Practice lesson. Ask participants to read either the elementary or secondary example on their own and as they read, highlight evidence of the Core Curriculum and the Curriculum of Practice.
- Divide the participants into an elementary group and a secondary group to share their thoughts about what they read.

Closure/Looking Forward

- Participants' upcoming task is to remodel or create quality lessons for a unit of study with the Curriculum of Practice Parallel as the focus. Distribute "Checklist for Designing Curriculum Within the Curriculum of Practice Parallel." Ask participants to use the checklist to examine strengths and weaknesses of a unit of study from their own or their district's curriculum. Suggest that for this activity they choose a unit they know quite well. If they prefer, they might return to the unit they designed to match the Core Curriculum. This would ensure that they begin with a solid unit, and can focus on ways they might adapt the unit to fit the Curriculum of Practice.
- Remind them of the symbol they developed in Workshop #1 to represent the Curriculum of Practice. Ask them if they wish to change or adapt this symbol.

NUTS AND BOLTS OF THE CURRICULUM OF PRACTICE PARALLEL

Intents/Purposes of the Curriculum of Practice

This parallel asks students to:

- Understand the nature of the discipline in a real-world application manner.
- Define and assume a role as a means of studying the discipline.

- Understand the impact of this discipline on other disciplines and other disciplines on this discipline.
- Become a disciplinary problem solver rather than being a problem solver using the subject matter of the discipline.
- Understand and use the discipline as a means of looking and making sense of the world.
- Develop a means of escaping the rut of certainty about knowledge.
- Comprehend the daily lives of workers or professionals in the discipline—working conditions, hierarchical structures, fiscal aspects of the work, and peer or collegial dynamics.
- Define and understand the implications of internal and external politics that impact the discipline.
- Value and engage in the intellectual struggle of the discipline.
- Function as a producer in the discipline.
- Function as a scholar in the discipline.

Adapted from *The Parallel Curriculum* (Tomlinson, et al., 2008) Figure 2.1.

Driving Questions of the Curriculum of Practice

- How do practitioner-scholars organize knowledge and skills in this discipline?
- How do practitioners use the discipline's concepts and principles in daily practice?
- What are the routine problems in the discipline?
- What strategies does a practitioner use to solve routine and nonroutine problems in the discipline?
- How does the practitioner know which skills to use under given circumstances?
- How does a practitioner sense when approaches and methods are ineffective in a given instance?
- What are the methods used by practitioners and contributors in the field to generate new questions, new knowledge, and solve problems?
- What are indicators of quality and success in the discipline?

Adapted from *The Parallel Curriculum* (Tomlinson, et al., 2008) Figure 6.1.

CURRICULUM OF PRACTICE AT WORK IN THE CLASSROOM

Middle School Example

Mrs. McQuerry is a middle school teacher who uses every opportunity she can to engage students in problem-based activities that introduce or extend the learning process in meaningful ways. She looks for newspaper and journal articles that highlight important concepts that her students are learning in their curriculum and tries to turn these ideas into problems for her students to solve. She has found that this way of teaching motivates her students and assists them in seeing the relevance of what they are learning to the reality of life. The project that her students worked on has been recently published in a book called *Nuclear Legacy: Students of Two Atomic Cities* (McQuerry, 2000).

This book was written by students from two communities: Richland, Washington, home of the Manhattan Project, and Slavutych, Ukraine, home for workers at the Chernobyl site. *Nuclear Legacy,* written in English and Ukrainian, is an example of authentic collaboration between cultures that captures a perspective on nuclear cultures seen from the first post—Cold

War generation and gives an insight into what may be possible for our global future as nuclear cultures now work together. Student perceptions of the history of their communities and hopes for the future of our world tell the nuclear story from the perspective of those who will inherit its legacy.

This project became a way to help Ukrainian and American students connect what they are learning in school to a real product that would be valuable outside the walls of the classroom. The book includes firsthand accounts by young people of the 1986 Chernobyl nuclear accident and interviews with scientists and engineers who worked on the 1940s Manhattan Project in the United States. In this book, students of two countries explore the history, present, and future of their nuclear communities and discuss with fresh voices their hopes for the future.

The study began in one semester elective course at Hanford Middle School in Richland, Washington, where students are given an opportunity to pursue a passion and given instruction in the inquiry method of research. This project was one of several conducted by the students. Each student is expected to become an active researcher by writing a project plan, taking and organizing notes, and conducting original research. The class culminates with a presentation before a committee of "experts."

In this class, Mrs. McQuerry provides guidance to students as they select projects of interest. Students interact with practicing professionals and design projects that require them to use the skills and modes of inquiry that fit particular disciplines. With the assistance of their teachers, the book students produce reflects new knowledge that is personally relevant to them and to their generation.

Adapted from *The Parallel Curriculum* (Tomlinson, et al., 2008) p. 170.

Elementary School Example

Mr. Harper's third grade class is studying the characteristics of organisms and have recently become intrigued by the earthworms they found on the playground after a recent rain shower. After visiting with the science coordinator at the school, Mr. Harper found out that she could order earthworms, egg cases, and baby earthworms from a biological supply company. This would allow his students to observe adult earthworms, the egg cases, the young earthworms, and some of the animals' characteristics.

While waiting for the earthworms to arrive, Mr. Harper took his students outside and asked them to make observations of the earthworms in their natural habitat. There he posed the questions, "If we wanted to study how earthworms behave, how would we set up an environment in our classroom that closely resembles the natural setting? This stimulated the students to gather library books from the library to draw plans for a simulated environment that would be arranged in the classroom.

After discussing their plans, the students decided to create a habitat for an earthworm by using a terrarium that was strategically placed away from the direct sunlight. The students covered the sides of the terrarium with black paper into which soil, leaves, and grass were added in the habitat. After the other earthworms arrived from the supply company, they were placed into the terrarium.

In the first weeks of instruction, students were asked to make any observations that would record how earthworms move, a description and illustration of what they look like, and what the students thought the earthworms were doing. They described the color and shape; they weighed and measured the earthworm, and designed large date charts to record their observations. The focus of their observation was mainly descriptive at this point.

As the unit progressed, students began to generate questions that Mr. Harper recorded on the chart. These questions were used to develop several explorations for the students to conduct. One group chose to investigate the life cycle of earthworms. They found several egg cases in the soil and this led them to books in the library that described the life cycle process. They were also interested in trying to figure out a way to keep track of the growth of a baby earthworm as it developed over time.

Three other groups of students were trying to investigate the types of environments the earthworms prefer. Mr. Harper suggested that they try different things like moisture and temperature and then coached them through the process of controlling variables. A fourth group was trying to decide what the earthworms like to eat. The students had read about the kinds of food the earthworms prefer and they now were just beginning to set up experiments to try to determine what they liked best. The last group was trying to set up a transparent environment for the earthworms so that they could study what earthworms do in various types of soil.

In this study and inquiry into the life of an earthworm, Mr. Harper's students learned about the basic needs of a particular organism, the basic structures and functions, the life cycle and some features of animal behavior. They simulated the role of a scientist by generating questions, planning and conducting experiments, measuring and recording data, identifying patterns in data, and reaching conclusions about some of the basic concepts and principles underlying the life sciences.

Adapted from *The Parallel Curriculum* (Tomlinson, et al., 2008) pp. 169–170.

CHECKLIST FOR DESIGNING CURRICULUM WITHIN THE CURRICULUM OF PRACTICE PARALLEL

To what degree is the unit designed to help students:

- Organize knowledge and skills in this discipline as practitioners and scholars do?
- Work as a scholar or practitioner of the discipline?
- Experience the routine—and nonroutine—problems of the discipline?
- Choose appropriate skills of the discipline for a given set of circumstances?
- Realize when to abandon an approach to problem solving as unproductive or inefficient?
- Generate new questions, new knowledge, and solve problems in the discipline?

Adapted from *The Parallel Curriculum* (Tomlinson, et al., 2008) Figure 2.1.

WORKSHOP #28

Content in the Curriculum of Practice Parallel

Session Objectives

In this session, participants frame a Curriculum of Practice unit of study by identifying the understandings (i.e., principles and generalizations), concepts, and skills for their targeted lessons or unit geared to the Curriculum of Practice. Encourage them to identify the skills and methodologies of scholars and practitioners in their discipline so they can work to include them in their unit content.

Masters

- Content Suggestions for the Curriculum of Practice

CONTENT SUGGESTIONS FOR THE CURRICULUM OF PRACTICE

- Consider which methodologies (tools, procedures, and skills) of a specific discipline would help students answer questions about a particular idea or to solve problems within a discipline; acquire and use information; analyze and organize data; and, reach conclusions.
- For example, in *science* the inquiry process relies on these skills:
  - Asking questions
  - Making observations
  - Setting up experiments
  - Refining and validating hypotheses
  - Drawing conclusions
- In *history*, historians use some of these skills and others to investigate the past:
  - Seeking evidence
  - Determining the authenticity of documents
  - Documenting bias
- Determine the types of questions, problems, or discrepant events that will be uncovered by students as they apply research methodologies.
- Consider how students will use the information they discover in their investigations to deepen their understanding of key principles and concepts and their relationships.
- Determine the types of problem-solving processes or modes of inquiry that will be used to solve problems or to investigate questions.
- Work with students to generate questions, determine the methodologies and procedures for carrying out the investigation, gather and analyze data, reach conclusions, and determine the implications of the research findings.
- Identify which habits of mind are to be developed through the use of this learning experience (e.g., independence, persistence, and dealing with ambiguity).
- Consider ethical issues or problems that can be used as subjects for the investigation.
- Identify the modes of inquiry that are listed in national standards documents.

Adapted from *The Parallel Curriculum* (Tomlinson, et al., 2008) Figure 6.4.

WORKSHOP #29

Assessment in the Curriculum of Practice Parallel

Session Objectives

This session provides opportunities for participants to (1) adjust the assessment components of their unit to match the intents and purposes of the Curriculum of Practice, (2) consider a continuum of expertise for the skills and methodologies of scholars and practitioners of a discipline, and (3) think about ways to encourage students to self-assess, a key skill of both the scholar and the practitioner.

Masters

- Assessment Suggestions for the Curriculum of Practice
- Scholarly Research Rubric
- Techniques for Ensuring High-Quality Self-Assessment for the Curriculum of Practice

ASSESSMENT SUGGESTIONS
FOR THE CURRICULUM OF PRACTICE

- Consider which methodologies (tools, procedures, and skills) of a specific discipline might assist students in answering their own research questions, probing the meaning of the key ideas of the discipline, and testing the adaptability of those ideas in other contexts.
- Determine the varying levels of sophistication, expertise, or technical proficiency in the use of methodological skills to assist learners toward continued growth (see "Scholarly Research Rubric").
- Consider how students will demonstrate their understanding in using the methodological skills, how their knowledge has changed over time, and the degree to which they interpret, apply, and transfer the knowledge and skills that they have gained to new contexts.
- Determine which products will be used to communicate new understandings and document growth.
- Consider a variety of products that can be used to show evidence of understanding of new ideas, new connections, transformation of existing ideas in new contexts, and flexibility in acquiring data.
- Provide ample opportunities for students to communicate their findings in a variety of formats.
- Observe and note changes in behavior (e.g., persistence, independence, and skepticism) over time.

Adapted from *The Parallel Curriculum* (Tomlinson, et al., 2008) Figure 6.4.

SCHOLARLY RESEARCH RUBRIC

Attributes	Distinguished	Apprentice	Naïve
Research Questions	Uses all questions to guide research; develops new questions to guide research	Uses most of the questions that were found interesting and testable; does not develop any new questions to research	Few, if any, questions are used to guide the study; does not develop any new questions to explore
Gathering Data	Uses a variety of resources; develops an accurate and extensive bibliography; uses sophisticated data gathering methods to further explore ideas	Uses many resources; developed an adequate bibliography; tries to revise their study, but experiences difficulty in carrying out research	Uses few resources; bibliography incomplete; does not revise research
Recording Data	Complete and accurate records, including supplementary data, are kept in notebooks and on data sheets	Complete and accurate records kept in notebooks	Records missing or incomplete from notebooks and data sheets

Attributes	Distinguished	Apprentice	Naïve
Analyzing Data	Skilled at using descriptive research methods to identify themes and make inferences	Developing a use of descriptive research methods to find themes and make inferences	Experiences difficulty using descriptive research to find themes and make inferences
Interpreting Findings	Explains data; accurate, logical explanations; sophisticated and thorough interpretation of events through perspective of those living in that setting; interpretations and explanations supported by data	Explains data; accurate, logical explanations; in-depth interpretation of events through perspective of those living in that setting	Poor or missing explanation of data; incomplete interpretation of historical events through perspective of those living in that setting
Reporting the Findings	Addresses most of the questions explored; inferences explained using found data; uses skills of evaluation as well as synthesis and analysis; supports claims with clear research evidence from valid sources	Addresses some of the questions explored; makes some inferences, though minor errors may exist; comprehension on inferential level and key skills are analysis and synthesis; supports some claims with research evidence	Addresses few questions explored; makes few inferences; weak inferences; answers deal with material on a concrete, literal level
Significance of the Findings	Makes meaning of information and incorporates it into own life by generating examples	Makes partial meaning of information and incorporates it into own life by generating examples	Makes little or no meaning of information and does not incorporate it into own life by generating examples
Conceptual Understanding	Identifies relationships between the concepts; change and perspective were sophisticated; might identify causal relationships between two concepts by providing examples; identifies relationships by moving beyond answering main question(s)	Identifies relationships that mostly focused on answers to main question(s) identified for research study; relationships that were explained are descriptive only	Identified relationships have little or no connection to questions
Products	Performance or product highly effective; ideas presented in engaging, polished, clear, and thorough manner; audience clearly in mind	Performance or product effective; ideas presented in clear and thorough manner; awareness of audience	Performance or product ineffective and unpolished providing little evidence of planning, practice, and consideration of audience

Adapted from *The Parallel Curriculum* (Tomlinson, et al., 2002) Figure 6.11.

TECHNIQUES FOR ENSURING HIGH-QUALITY
SELF-ASSESSMENT FOR THE CURRICULUM OF PRACTICE

- Provide students with working models that illustrate how professionals in various disciplines use certain skills and research methodologies to:
  - ○ Construct new knowledge in their fields.
  - ○ Extend their understandings about a particular topic or idea.
- Engage students in generating questions, selecting the methodologies and procedures for carrying out the investigation, gathering and analyzing data, reaching conclusions, and determining the implications of their research findings.
- Help students understand the evaluation criteria, which includes varying levels of sophistication, expertise, or technical proficiency in the use of methodological skills.
- Ask students to share their work with professional audiences.
- Offer product options that are as authentic to the discipline as practical.

Possible Self-Assessment Questions

- How does what I found match or conflict with what other scholars have discovered?
- What did it take to complete this project?
- Were there other questions that surfaced as I studied this topic or problem?
- What are the implications of my research?
- What new questions do I have regarding this inquiry?
- What kinds of questions does this discipline answer in terms of my life?
- What skills do I need further work on?
- What did my research reveal?

WORKSHOP #30

Introductory Activities in the Curriculum of Practice Parallel

---

Session Overview

In the beginning of a Curriculum of Practice unit, educators must plan opportunities for introducing students to the skills and dispositions used by practitioners and scholars in a particular discipline so that they too can understand what it takes to pursue this type of work. The purpose of these introductory activities is to establish a classroom environment that promotes active inquiry in students.

Masters

- Introductory Activity Suggestions for the Curriculum of Practice

---

INTRODUCTORY ACTIVITY SUGGESTIONS
FOR THE CURRICULUM OF PRACTICE

- Use focusing questions, problems, dilemmas, and discrepant events to justify the need for methodological skills.
- Identify experts who can assist students in identifying problems, developing technical expertise in the use of inquiry skills, and knowing which tools and procedures to use to best address these problems.

Adapted from *The Parallel Curriculum* (Tomlinson, et al., 2008) Figure 6.4.

WORKSHOP #31

Teaching Strategies in the Curriculum of Practice Parallel

Session Objectives

The Curriculum of Practice places a premium on those teaching methods that are more inductive and more inquiry-based in accordance with the goal of developing behaviors used by practitioners and scholars. Therefore the methods of teaching should put the learner in the role of a scholar or an inquirer in each subject or discipline area that is taught.

Masters

• Teaching Strategy Suggestions for the Curriculum of Practice

TEACHING STRATEGY SUGGESTIONS FOR THE CURRICULUM OF PRACTICE

- Develop a repertoire of teaching strategies that are more inductive and more inquiry-based in accordance with the goal of developing behaviors used by scholars (e.g., investigative studies, problem-based learning, independent studies, Socratic questioning, small and large group investigations, and simulations).
- Adjust and match teaching methods to the learners as they demonstrate continued growth in using the tools and procedures of the professional.

Adapted from *The Parallel Curriculum* (Tomlinson, et al., 2008) Figure 6.4.

WORKSHOP #32

Learning Activities in the Curriculum of Practice Parallel

Session Objectives

Learning activities in the Curriculum of Practice should ask students to use the strategies, methods, and procedures of the discipline to acquire information. Students should also learn to use the research process to complete more complex tasks within the discipline. Certain creative and analytical thinking skills are also well suited to the goals of this parallel. Encourage participants to incorporate learning activities that encourage growth in these skills as well.

It is important to consider the cognitive and affective developmental levels of the students for whom the learning activities are designed. Not all students will be ready to function as practitioners of a discipline. In some cases, a student indeed will be ready to *assume* the role of an expert practitioner whereas another student will be ready only to *simulate* the role of an expert practitioner. For an example of simulating the role of an expert practitioner, review the elementary school example about Mr. Harper's class under "Curriculum

(Continued)

(Continued)

of Practice at Work in the Classroom." For an example of becoming an expert practitioner, review the middle school example about Mrs. McQuerry's class under "Curriculum of Practice at Work in the Classroom."

Masters

- Learning Activity Suggestions for the Curriculum of Practice
- Critical and Creative Thinking Skills

LEARNING ACTIVITY SUGGESTIONS FOR THE CURRICULUM OF PRACTICE

- Make sure that the learning activities are those that provide opportunities for students to use the tools of the professional to acquire new information, enhance learning, and engage in research.
- Select activities that target the development of essential principles and concepts, or encourage the inquiry process.
- Introduce students to the inquiry process or steps to research.
- Acquire tools and technologies to advance the level of research that students conduct (e.g., probes and sensors, statistical software, word processor, data collection devices).
- Use graphing techniques to analyze data.

Adapted from *The Parallel Curriculum* (Tomlinson, et al., 2008) Figure 6.4.

CRITICAL AND CREATIVE THINKING SKILLS

Type of Thinking Skills	Student Examples
Information-Processing Skills Students locate and collect relevant information to sort, classify, sequence, compare and contrast, and analyze part to whole relationships.	• Ask students to write their home addresses. Ask each child to draw a map of the route from home to the classroom and describe the route to a partner. Discuss with the children who lives the farthest away and who lives the nearest. • With the children's help, design and carry out a survey of how children come to school. Help students use the information to draw a graph, which can be computer generated, and analyze the findings. • Have students observe and take photographs in the local community. Using these photographs, students research the history behind the locations. Conduct interviews with local residents to gain historical information about the community.
Reasoning Skills Students provide reasons for opinions and actions, draw inferences and make deductions, use precise language to explain what they think, and make judgments and decisions informed by reasons and/or evidence.	• Using the data collected in the activities listed above, have students design a historical walking tour map of the area. Students will make recommendations of places to see, describe their historical relevance, and add pictures of historical statues or sculptures that merit recognition. • Present these recommendations and the tour guide to an audience, such as a local historical museum.

Type of Thinking Skills	Student Examples
Inquiry Skills Students ask relevant questions, pose and define problems, plan what to do and ways to research, predict outcomes and anticipate consequences, and test conclusions and improve ideas.	• Arrange for the children to complete a simple traffic survey on the road outside the school. With the children's help, label a wall display of photographs of the road outside the school to show aspects related to traffic (e.g., road signs, road markings). • Ask the children to think about their own road at home and decide whether it is quieter or noisier than the school road. Encourage the children to think up their own questions about traffic around the school. Discuss with the children what makes a "fair" test in a survey (e.g., times, frequency, place). With the children's help, design and carry out a survey of the numbers of cars parked in the street. Ask the children to present the results as a graph, using simple graphing software, and analyze the results. Ask the children to consider questions like: Are the parked cars there all day? Where do people go when they park their cars?
Creative Thinking Skills Students generate and extend ideas, suggest hypotheses, apply imagination, and look for alternative innovative outcomes or solutions.	• Ask the children to identify methods of making an area safe (e.g., bicycle paths, pavements, fencing, "no parking" zones, road signs, pedestrian crossings) and to think about how the school grounds and other streets they know are made safe. • Ask the children to make use of all the evidence they have collected (photographs and survey results) to write a letter to the transportation department at the local council to ask about the possibility of a safety feature (e.g., a pedestrian crossing) being constructed.
Evaluation Skills Students evaluate information; judge the value of what they read, hear, and observe; develop criteria for judging the value of their own and others' work or ideas; and provide reasons for their decision.	• Students will discuss the pros and cons of building a hotel near a small coastal region. • Divide the children into five groups, each assuming one of the following roles: fisherman, local government official, travel company representative, store owner, and local resident. • Students will first work in small groups with peers portraying the same role to develop information and prepare statements that support their viewpoints about building the hotel. • Next, new groupings will be formed, this time composed of one representative from each role group. In these new groups, all participants will listen to, take notes on, and discuss the varying viewpoints on the hotel project. • After students have had a chance to revise their statements, the class will stage a mock public hearing on the hotel project. A vote will be taken to determine the outcome.

Adapted from *The Parallel Curriculum* (Tomlinson, et al., 2008) Figure 6.5.

WORKSHOP #33

Grouping Practices in the Curriculum of Practice Parallel

Session Objectives

In this parallel, students should learn how to assume the role of the professional. Professionals must work independently as well as collaboratively, and learn to self-regulate their work. It is to be expected that students of all ages vary greatly in their readiness for the skills of collaboration, independent work, and self-assessment. At some points in a unit, a teacher may need to work with the whole class to teach such skills. Sometimes teachers will work with small groups of students who need to hone specific skills. At other times, students may work alone or with peers to practice or perfect their skills.

The "Student Planning Record" provides an illustration of a simple format that students might use to track and support their growth in these areas. Journals and group planning sheets can also be used to document their progress.

Masters

• Grouping Suggestions for the Curriculum of Practice
• Student Planning Record

GROUPING SUGGESTIONS
FOR THE CURRICULUM OF PRACTICE

Employ a variety of grouping arrangements (flexible, small group, individual, interest-based, across grade levels, multiaged) based on students' readiness levels, learning styles, skill accomplishment, and the goals of lessons based on the Curriculum of Practice. Be mindful of what a practitioner's goals for any endeavor might be and select grouping strategies accordingly.

Adapted from *The Parallel Curriculum* (Tomlinson, et al., 2008) Figure 6.4.

STUDENT PLANNING RECORD

Name _____ **Inquiry** _____

Date _____ **Class** _____

The tasks I worked on today:

Activity	Completion

Evaluation:

_____ I completed my goals.

_____ I used my time wisely.

Next time, I plan to:

Activity	Materials or resources I will need

Adapted from *The Parallel Curriculum* (Tomlinson, et al., 2008) Figure 6.7.

WORKSHOP #34

Resources in the Curriculum of Practice Parallel

Session Objectives

Resources in a Curriculum of Practice unit probably include those that are used by practicing professionals in a variety of disciplines. Resources may also include the equipment or tools that are used by scholars in the field to conduct their research.

Masters

• Resources Suggestions for the Curriculum of Practice

RESOURCES SUGGESTIONS FOR THE CURRICULUM OF PRACTICE

- Locate methodological tools that can be used to collect data.
- Identify community experts who can help students learn the skills and methodologies used in various disciplines.
- Locate videos, books, artifacts, photographs, artwork, electronic information, community members, experts in the field, primary and second source documents, and methodological guides (how-to books) to support student research.

Adapted from *The Parallel Curriculum* (Tomlinson, et al., 2008) Figure 6.4.

WORKSHOP #35

Products in the Curriculum of Practice Parallel

Session Objectives

In a Curriculum of Practice unit, students should be provided with opportunities to select those products that resemble the work of scholars and that best match where the students are in terms of readiness, interest, and learning preferences.

It is also important for students working in this parallel to present their product to a significant audience—those who are interested in the students' work, those who might benefit from the results of the students' findings, and those who can provide expertlike evaluations that can assist students in improving upon their knowledge, understanding, ideas, working processes, and skills.

Masters

- Product Suggestions for the Curriculum of Practice

PRODUCT SUGGESTIONS FOR THE CURRICULUM OF PRACTICE

- Determine the variety of products that can be used to provide evidence of increased understanding of the principles and concepts in a particular field, research procedures, and new discoveries made about an area of study.
- Select the types of products that are close approximations of the types of products that practicing professionals create in their fields (e.g., gallery displays, documentaries, books, articles, social action plans, compositions, and scientific studies).
- Consider audiences that can best provide students with authentic evaluation of their work.

Adapted from *The Parallel Curriculum* (Tomlinson, et al., 2008) Figure 6.4.

WORKSHOP #36

Extensions in the Curriculum of Practice Parallel

Session Objectives

The inquiry-based learning activities of this parallel often lead to other questions to be studied in current or other subject-area classes and thus can provide the basis for extension activities. Extensions can be designed to have students interact or work with researchers, college professors, or community experts who can provide methodological support and assistance to the students. When possible, teachers can ask writers, archaeologists, sociologists, biologists, mathematicians, and community members for assistance in creating such opportunities for students. These professionals can help generate problem-based experiences, provide methodological guidance in helping students learn the procedures to conduct research, to write books, to graphically illustrate important ideas, etc., or even provide the resources and materials students need to conduct investigations.

Masters

- Extension Activity Suggestions for the Curriculum of Practice

EXTENSION ACTIVITY SUGGESTIONS
FOR THE CURRICULUM OF PRACTICE

- Listen carefully for questions that students raise prior to, during, and after instruction.
- Consider community experts who can provide advanced technical assistance to those students who are ready.
- Determine other areas in which students want to explore, practice, or apply newly acquired skills of practice.

Adapted from *The Parallel Curriculum* (Tomlinson, et al., 2008) Figure 6.4.

WORKSHOP #37

Differentiation and AID in the Curriculum of Practice Parallel

Session Objectives

As in the other parallels, student variance in terms of readiness, interests, and learning preferences must also be addressed in the Curriculum of Practice. Furthermore, as students become more expertlike, teachers may need to employ strategies of Ascending Intellectual Demand (AID) in order to ensure continuous intellectual ascent in these students.

Masters

- Differentiation and AID Suggestions for the Curriculum of Practice
- AID and the Curriculum of Practice Parallel

DIFFERENTIATION AND AID SUGGESTIONS
FOR THE CURRICULUM OF PRACTICE

- Provide opportunities for students to guide their own inquiries.
- Devise tasks and products that cause students to develop, through application, personal frameworks of knowledge, understanding, and skill related to the discipline.
- Increase the difficulty level and authenticity of resource materials that are used by the students during their research.
- Identify new contexts for transferring and applying knowledge.
- Guide students in establishing their own goals for work at what they believe to be the next steps of research and in quality for their own growth; assess work according to those standards.
- Escalate the level of analysis for the investigation.
- Network students with mentors in the field to advance their knowledge and research skills.
- Use the parallel's guidelines for AID in selecting resources and designing learning activities and products.

Adapted from *The Parallel Curriculum* (Tomlinson, et al., 2008) Figure 6.4.

AID AND THE CURRICULUM OF PRACTICE PARALLEL

- Encourage students to distinguish between approaches that seem relevant in tackling authentic problems of the discipline and those that are less relevant.
- Call on students to develop a language of reflection about problems and scenarios in the field.
- Devise tasks and products that cause students to develop, through application, personal frameworks of knowledge, understanding, and skill related to the discipline.
- Have students test those frameworks through repeated field-based tasks and refine them as necessary.
- Have students compare standards of quality used by practitioners, connoisseurs, and critics in the field to standards of quality typically used in school as they relate to problem solving in that field.
- Guide students in establishing their own goals for work at what they believe to be the next steps in quality for their own growth and to assess their own work according to those standards.
- Make it possible for students to submit best-quality exemplars of their own work to experts in a field for expert-level feedback.
- Have students work on problems currently posing difficulties for experts in the discipline.
- Structure products and tasks to require students to engage in persistent, prolonged, written reflection about their own work and thinking in the field, with analysis and critique of those patterns as they evolve.
- Call on students to compare and contrast their own approaches to discipline-based dilemmas, issues, or problems with those of experts in the field.

Adapted from *The Parallel Curriculum* (Tomlinson, et al., 2008) Figure 6.8.

WORKSHOP #38

Closure in the Curriculum of Practice Parallel

Session Objectives

In the Curriculum of Practice, teachers use lesson and unit closure activities to help focus students on their work as practitioners in the discipline. Strategies such as comparison and contrast charts, analysis of expert rubrics, use of minibiographies of experts, and whole class and small group discussions can help the teacher focus students on vocabulary and methodology of a discipline; use of concepts, principles, and essential questions to guide problem finding and problem solving; investigating experts' habits of mind and work; dealing with fuzzy, complex, and often intractable problems and issues; and evaluating outcomes of their work as practitioners. Focusing questions for the Parallel of Practice can be very helpful in framing lesson and unit closure activities.

Masters

- Closure Suggestions for the Curriculum of Practice

CLOSURE SUGGESTIONS FOR THE CURRICULUM OF PRACTICE

- Help students focus on essential questions, methods used to seek answers to those questions, and the degree to which their methods were fruitful.
- Guide students in thinking about how concepts and principles informed their thinking.
- Ask students to reflect on which knowledge they used in their work and how they knew it was (or wasn't) useful in their thinking and problem solving.
- Have students compare their experience as practitioners with experiences of experts in the discipline about whom they are learning.
- Ask students to reflect on their work and products using expert-level rubrics, standards, or indicators of quality.
- Ensure that students use the vocabulary of method, thought, and habits of mind and work that experts would use.
- Help students articulate how they approached issues that are complex and/or have ethical implications.

Adapted from *The Parallel Curriculum* (Tomlinson, et al., 2008) Figure 6.4.

Note to Facilitator

As you progress through subsequent sessions, continue to lead participants through each key component as you did in the previous parallels. Like before, you will introduce and discuss a curriculum component and provide suggestions on how to make that component take on the flavor of the Parallel of Identity. After each component is featured, allow time for participants to remodel or create lessons so they are in alignment with the Curriculum of Identity. As with the chapter devoted to the Curriculum of Practice, for the sessions devoted to each curriculum component, you have only been provided with objectives and list of masters for each component. Continue to use solid teaching methodologies as you work with participants (see Appendix A). Keep in mind that by this point in the series of workshops, some may move faster than others through the components. Others will prefer to look at their unit design in a more holistic fashion. Don't feel absolutely tied to following the sequence of components as presented. There may be participants who just want to be given the set of handouts for this parallel and go on from there.

The Curriculum of Identity Parallel

Note to Facilitator

To prepare for the workshops in this chapter, you may wish to review Chapter 7 of the Parallel Curriculum Model, "The Curriculum of Identity Parallel" in *The Parallel Curriculum* by Tomlinson, et al. (2008).

WORKSHOP #39

The Curriculum of Identity Parallel

Session Overview

This session focuses on the basic tenets of the Curriculum of Identity, specifically its definition, intent, benefits, and driving questions.

Masters

- A Metaphor for the Curriculum of Identity
- Nuts and Bolts of the Curriculum of Identity Parallel
- Curriculum of Identity at Work in the Classroom
- Checklist for Designing Curriculum Within the Curriculum of Identity Parallel

Session Details

Introduction

- First, review with participants that there are four ways of approaching curriculum. Explain that the focus for this session is to understand the purpose, intent, and driving questions associated with the Curriculum of Identity parallel and then directly apply what they learn to remodeling a chosen lesson(s) or unit to be in alignment with this parallel. Reintroduce the "The Parallel Curriculum" (Workshop #1) and draw attention to the fourth parallel—the *Curriculum of Identity*.

- Post the following questions based on the driving questions of the Curriculum of Identity and ask participants to discuss them in small groups.
  - ○ How do educators think and work? How do I like to think and work?
  - ○ What are the problems and issues on which educators spend their lives? To what degree are these intriguing to me?
  - ○ What difficulties do educators encounter? How have they coped with the difficulties? How do I cope with them?
  - ○ What are the ethical principles at the core of the discipline? How are those like and unlike my ethics?
  - ○ How do people in this discipline handle ambiguity, uncertainty, persistence, failure, success, collaboration, and compromise? How do I handle those things?
  - ○ What is the wisdom this discipline has contributed to the world? How has that affected me? To what degree can I see myself contributing to that wisdom?

Teaching and Learning Activities

- Ask participants to imagine themselves at a department store in front of a three-way mirror. Share "A Metaphor for the Curriculum of Identity."

Ask: "What do *you* see when you look in such a "disciplinary mirror"? To what degree does who *you* are match the identity of a scholar or practitioner in your discipline (e.g., historian, scientist, writer, musician)?"

- Distribute and discuss "Nuts and Bolts of the Curriculum of Identity Parallel."

Say: "The Curriculum of Identity Parallel is designed to help students see themselves in relation to the discipline both now and with possibilities for the future; understand the discipline more fully by connecting it with their lives and experiences; increase awareness of their preferences, strengths, interests, and need for growth; and think about themselves as stewards of the discipline who may contribute to it and/or through it.

"The Curriculum of Identity uses curriculum as a catalyst for self-definition and self-understanding, with the belief that by looking outward to the discipline, students can find a means of looking inward. A focus on the concepts and principles of the discipline ensures that the Core Curriculum remains embedded within this parallel and moves beyond a purely affective curriculum."

- Distribute "Curriculum of Identity at Work in the Classroom." This gives a brief overview of what two teachers did with a Curriculum of Identity lesson. Ask participants to read either the elementary or secondary example on their own and as they read, highlight evidence of the Core Curriculum and/or the Curriculum of Identity.
- Divide the participants into an elementary group and a secondary group to share their thoughts about what they read.

Closure/Looking Forward

- Participants' upcoming task is to remodel or create quality lessons for a unit of study with the Curriculum of Identity Parallel as the focus. Distribute "Checklist for Designing Curriculum Within the Curriculum of Identity Parallel." Ask participants to use the checklist to examine strengths and weaknesses of a unit of study from their own or their district's curriculum. Suggest that for this activity they choose a unit they know quite well. If they prefer, they might return to the unit they designed to match the Core Curriculum. This would ensure that they begin with a solid unit, and can focus on ways they might adapt the unit to fit the Curriculum of Identity.
- Remind participants of the symbol they developed in Workshop #1 to represent the Curriculum of Identity. Ask them if they wish to change or adapt this symbol.

A METAPHOR FOR THE CURRICULUM OF IDENTITY PARALLEL

The Curriculum of Identity may best be understood using the metaphor of a three-way mirror:

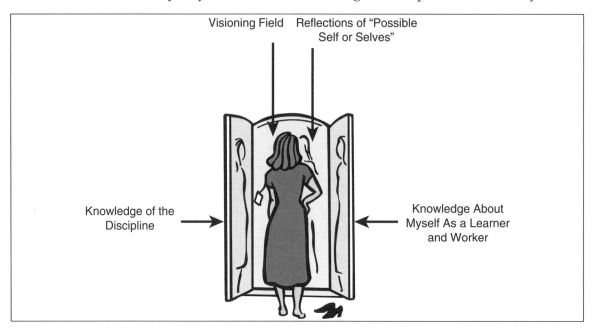

Adapted from *The Parallel Curriculum* (Tomlinson, et al., 2008) Figure 7.1.

In this image, the mirror is a metaphor for the feedback provided by teachers, teaching and learning activities, and experts in the targeted field, as well as the student himself or herself.

- The panel on the left represents a student's *knowledge of the discipline.*
- The panel on the right represents a student's *knowledge about the self as a learner and worker.*
- The center panel is the *visioning field* and presents students with *reflections of possible self or selves.* This panel offers opportunities for students to assess the "degree of fit" between themselves and the discipline, both now and in the future and "correct their course" in response to questions such as:
  o Do I like what I am learning?
  o Who are the professionals who use this information in their daily lives?
  o Would I want to become like these professionals?
- Depending on answers to these questions and many others like them, students will be either satisfied and continue with their original orientation or unsatisfied with the fit and make modifications to their life course.

NUTS AND BOLTS OF THE CURRICULUM OF IDENTITY PARALLEL

Intents/Purposes of the Curriculum of Identity

This parallel asks students to:

- Reflect on their skills and interests as they relate to the discipline.
- Understand ways in which their interests might be useful to the discipline and ways in which the discipline might serve as a means for helping them develop their skills and interests.

- Develop awareness of their modes of working as they relate to the modes of operation characteristics of the discipline.
- Reflect on the impact of the discipline in the world and of self in the discipline.
- Think about the impact of the discipline on the lives of others in the wider world.
- Take intellectual samplings of the discipline for the purpose of experiencing self in relation to the discipline.
- Examine the ethics and philosophy characteristic of the discipline and their implications.
- Project themselves into the discipline.
- Develop self in the context of the discipline and through interaction with the subject matter.
- Develop a sense of both pride and humility related to both self and the discipline.

Adapted from *The Parallel Curriculum* (Tomlinson, et al., 2008) Figure 2.1.

Driving Questions of the Curriculum of Identity

- What do practitioners and contributors in this discipline think about?
- To what degree is this familiar, surprising, and/or intriguing to me?
- When I am intrigued by an idea, what do I gain from that, what do I give as a result of that, and what difference does it make?
- How do people in this discipline think and work?
- In what ways do those processes seem familiar, surprising, or intriguing to me?
- What are the problems and issues on which practitioners and contributors in this discipline spend their lives?
- To what degree are those intriguing to me?
- What is the range of vocational and avocational possibilities in this discipline?
- In which ones can I see myself working?
- What difficulties do practitioners and contributors in this discipline encounter?
- How have they coped with the difficulties?
- How do I think I would cope with them?
- What are the ethical principles at the core of the discipline?
- How are those like and unlike my ethics?
- Who have been the "heroes" of the evolving discipline?
- What are the attributes of these "heroes"?
- What do I learn about myself by studying them?
- Who have been the "villains" of the evolving discipline?
- What are the attributes of these "villains"?
- What do I learn about myself by studying them?
- How do people in this discipline handle ambiguity, uncertainty, persistence, failure, success, collaboration, and compromise?
- How do I handle those things?
- What is the wisdom this discipline has contributed to the world?
- How has that affected me?
- To what degree can I see myself contributing to that wisdom?
- How might I shape the discipline, and how might it shape me?

Adapted from *The Parallel Curriculum* (Tomlinson, et al., 2008) Figure 7.3.

CURRICULUM OF IDENTITY AT WORK IN THE CLASSROOM

Secondary Example

In Mrs. Mitchell's eleventh grade English class, writing is a centerpiece of the curriculum. All students work to meet certain prescribed writing standards, and all students regularly take part in writing process workshops. Students also select a kind of writing for further exploration. Amy and Darius selected a genre in which they have a personal interest: Amy is a writer of short stories and novels, and Darius is a playwright.

Amy and Darius will study writers relevant to their preferred genres, looking at how these people became writers, how their careers have evolved over time, what has been positive for them in their writing lives and what has been costly, what advice they give aspiring writers, and particularly how their writings reflect the authors' cultures, values, and world views. The overarching question Amy and Darius are addressing is "What does it mean to be a writer?" Ultimately, they each will develop a way of answering this question as it relates to the writers they have studied and to themselves as present and future writers. Their reflections will be crafted in the genre(s) they share and the group of writers investigated. Ultimately, the two students should have a fuller sense of what it means for others to be writers but also ways in which the pursuit of writing is (or is not) a good match for their own interests, habits, perspectives, and temperaments. They should also develop insights into ways in which the pursuit of writing might contribute to their own lives and ways in which they might contribute to writing as a field.

Elementary Example

Mr. Yin is working for six weeks in a resource room for students identified as gifted. All of the students have a keen interest in history. In their regular classroom, they are currently studying the period leading up to the Civil War. Their resource room curriculum will guide them in thinking about the Underground Railroad as a way of understanding themselves and the period more fully. Students will read from a variety of both primary and secondary sources to understand perspectives of slaves, freed slaves, slave owners, Northerners opposed to slavery, and other groups during the pre–Civil War time.

Students will keep a journal with three sections. In one section, they will record ideas, information, and conclusions as a historian would, trying to use data to present a verifiable and balanced view of events. In a second section, they will write from the perspective of a person in a role they are assigned and on whom they do research (e.g., a slave or an abolitionist). In the third section, they will write about their own thoughts and feelings on the period and people they are learning about, the work and responsibilities of a historian, and courage across time, including courage demonstrated in their own lives.

At the end of their study, students will participate in panel discussions among members of various groups from the pre–Civil War era, historians who chronicled the period, and contemporary students. They will discuss what people can learn from the period, how people can have confidence in what they learn, and how people can shape their lives with what they learn from history.

Adapted from *The Parallel Curriculum* (Tomlinson, et al., 2002), pp. 40–41.

CHECKLIST FOR DESIGNING CURRICULUM WITHIN THE CURRICULUM OF IDENTITY PARALLEL

To what degree is the unit designed to help students:

- Sample the discipline in order to understand themselves in relation to it?
- Develop an appreciation of the potential of one or more disciplines to help people—including themselves—make sense of their world and live more satisfying and productive lives?
- Reflect on and identify their skills, interests, and talents as they relate to one or more disciplines?
- Understand how they might shape and be shaped by ongoing participation in a discipline?
- Develop a clear sense of what types of lives practitioners and contributors to a discipline lead on a day-to-day, as well as on a long-term, basis?
- Explore the positive and negative impacts of the discipline on the lives of people and circumstances in the world?
- Examine their own interests, ways of thinking, ways of working, values, ethics, philosophy, norms, and definitions of quality by examining those things as reflected in the discipline?
- Understand the excitement that people in a discipline have about ideas, issues, problems, and so on, and how those things energize contributors to a discipline?
- Understand the role of self-discipline in practitioners and contributors to the discipline and reflect on their own evolving self-discipline?
- Think about how creativity is visible in the discipline and about their own creativity?
- Develop a sense of pride and a sense of humility related to self and the discipline?

Adapted from *The Parallel Curriculum* (Tomlinson, et al., 2008) p. 29.

WORKSHOP #40

Content in the Curriculum of Identity Parallel

Session Objectives

In this session, participants will frame a unit of study by identifying the understandings (principles/generalizations), concepts, and skills for targeted lessons or a unit geared to the Curriculum of Identity.

In addition to teaching to cognitive standards, this parallel works to support identity formation among young people by identifying a list of affective goals to incorporate into unit design as well. A list of such goals is included in "Affective Goals for the Curriculum of Identity." Participants will want to include some of these goals in the content component of their curriculum.

Masters

- Affective Goals of the Curriculum of Identity
- Content Suggestions for the Curriculum of Identity

AFFECTIVE GOALS OF THE CURRICULUM OF IDENTITY

Self-Esteem

The student:

- Believes in own self-worth and maintains a positive view of self.
- Demonstrates knowledge of own skills and abilities.
- Is aware of impact on others.
- Knows own emotional capacity and needs and how to address them.

Sociability

The student:

- Demonstrates understanding, friendliness, adaptability, empathy, and politeness in new and ongoing group settings.
- Asserts self in familiar and unfamiliar social situations.
- Relates well to others.
- Responds appropriately as the situation requires.
- Takes an interest in what others say and do.

Self-Management

The student:

- Assesses own knowledge, skills, and abilities accurately.
- Sets well-defined and realistic personal goals.
- Monitors progress toward goal attainment and motivates self through goal achievement.
- Exhibits self-control and responds to feedback unemotionally and nondefensively.
- Is a self-starter (U.S. Department of Labor, 1992).
- Will assume primary responsibility for learning, including identifying their needs and setting reasonable goals (Connecticut State Department of Education, 1998).

Adapted from *The Parallel Curriculum* (Tomlinson, et al., 2008) p. 203.

CONTENT SUGGESTIONS FOR THE CURRICULUM OF IDENTITY

- Determine the concepts, principles, skills, methodologies, and dispositions (e.g., interests, attitudes, beliefs, and expression style preferences) of practicing professionals in the discipline you will teach.
- Consider objectives from the Secretary's Commission on Achieving Necessary Skills (SCANS) Report (U.S. Department of Labor, 1992), which address essential workplace skills.
- Target the concepts, principles, skills, methodologies, and dispositions from the world of the practicing professionals that best match the goals and purposes of the curriculum unit.
- Work with students to gather and analyze data from their learning and work profiles

- Create charts that display the students' learning and work profiles. Identify patterns and trends in the class profile. Make note of individual profiles as well.
- Make appropriate accommodations in the unit to address patterns in students' learning and work profiles (e.g., address students' interests, encourage students' opportunities to work in their preferred learning or expression style) and to reflect consistently on what they learn about themselves through their work.

Adapted from *The Parallel Curriculum* (Tomlinson, et al., 2008) Figure 7.4.

WORKSHOP #41

Assessment in the Curriculum of Identity Parallel

Session Objectives

To align assessment tasks with the goals and purposes of the Curriculum of Identity, teachers likely will remodel assessments so that they require student reflection, address the need for student choice, encourage self reflection on the part of practitioners or student practitioners, and/or use longitudinal rubrics that address the talent development process and help visualize student growth over time.

Masters

- Assessment Suggestions for the Curriculum of Identity
- Sample Assessments in the Curriculum of Identity
- Longitudinal Rubric: Historian

ASSESSMENT SUGGESTIONS FOR THE CURRICULUM OF IDENTITY

- Create longitudinal rubrics to identify the stages of talent development in students in a variety of content areas. Use the rubric to note the evolution of student abilities in the classroom, determine where each student is on the novice to expert continuum, and decide on strategies that can be used to guide the student to the next level of proficiency.
- Use assessment formats that require student reflection (e.g., goal statements, reflective essays, longitudinal portfolios, journals, photographic essays that chronicle a student's passage from novice toward expert, and personal discoveries).
- Provide students with time to document and analyze their own learning and work profile over time and identify emerging patterns and trends.
- Provide a choice in assessment tasks to accommodate student preferences.
- Ensure systematic opportunities for students to reflect on their past, present, and future selves throughout their K–12 experience.
- Share with parents or a significant adult where each child is in his or her development. Explore with them the ways that they can contribute to development of student interests and abilities at home.

Adapted from *The Parallel Curriculum* (Tomlinson, et al., 2008) Figure 7.4.

SAMPLE ASSESSMENTS IN THE CURRICULUM OF IDENTITY

Elementary: How Much Is a Million?

Think about:

— A favorite object, like a toy or a piece of sports equipment;
— A favorite food, like M&M's or gum drops; OR,
— A favorite activity, like shooting baskets or jumping rope.

Using a calculator, choose *one* of the following and tell me:

- How much 1,000,000 of your objects might weigh.
- How long 1,000,000 of your objects would be lined up side by side.
- How tall 1,000,000 of your objects might be when stacked one on top of the other.
- How long it might take you to complete your favorite activity 1,000,000 times.

Write about your findings or draw a picture to illustrate your answers.

Secondary: Essay Prompt

Identify the personal sacrifices Robert Frost made in his evolution as a poet and why he was willing to make them. Then, explain the personal sacrifices you would be willing to make to achieve a similar level of accomplishment in your selected field. In what ways are your goals and willingness to sacrifice to reach them like and unlike Robert Frost's?

Self Assessment

- What did I learn?
- What was easy for me?
- How might I describe my strength(s)?
- What was still confusing for me?
- What questions do I have that might clear up my confusion?
- Who might help me?
- What aspects were particularly interesting?
- Would I like to continue doing this kind of work in the discipline? Why or why not?

Adapted from *The Parallel Curriculum* (Tomlinson, et al., 2008) Figure 7.5.

LONGITUDINAL RUBRIC: HISTORIAN

	Student Behavior	*Possible Action to Encourage Talent Development*
1	Jose asks numerous questions about people and events from the past.	Read books to Jose about famous historical people; share historical book titles with parents so they can read to student, too.
2	As a seven year old, Jose spends twenty minutes longer than any of his first grade peers looking at a diorama depicting the Battle of Lexington and Concord.	Investigate local and regional historical sites; provide Jose's parents with names of some sites so they can visit them as a family.

	Student Behavior	Possible Action to Encourage Talent Development
3	When offered the opportunity, Jose enjoys visiting historical sites, touching historical artifacts, and reading nonfiction and fiction texts about historical topics.	Help Jose gather information about historical sites and artifacts; enlist the support of the library media specialist to get additional resources for him.
4	When given options about projects (e.g., writing or reading assignments), Jose generally chooses alternatives that address some aspect of history.	Provide extension activities for Jose on topics that he enjoys; suggest other related directions that he may find equally, or even more, appealing.
5	As a young adolescent, Jose is beginning to make a conscious effort to attend classes, read books and, in general, increase his knowledge and skills about historical topics and methods.	Discuss the discipline of history with Jose; talk about the methodology of the field; explore course offerings; encourage Jose's parents to work with the guidance counselor to select appropriate history courses.
6	Jose prefers and seeks out the company of peers who also enjoy history. He likes working with these students on class projects. He volunteers his time in community projects that address historical issues or needs.	Use community resources to uncover projects and issues related to history; use the Internet to locate other resources and projects.
7	Jose begins to realize that he might be a future historian. While he enjoys every aspect of his studies and work in history, he senses that he has much to learn to become a practitioner.	Locate internships for Jose that will provide him with an in-depth look at the skills and methodologies required of historians.
8	Jose begins to make short-term and long-term plans for professional growth. Often, he forgoes leisure activities in order to advance his personal and professional expertise.	Locate a mentorship for Jose. Look for regionally or nationally based organizations that have members like Jose, such as historical societies; encourage Jose to become a member.
9	Jose is thinking and working like a professional; he is developing a knack for finding interesting questions, unexplored topics, discrepant information, and controversies in history.	Encourage and support Jose's frequently intense work on topics that compel him. Assist with resource acquisition. Enlist professionals to advise him and provide feedback on the nature and quality of his work.
10	Jose enjoys his association with colleagues who like to discuss abstract ideas, who enjoy unearthing unanswered questions, and who derive satisfaction from exploring possible answers to unanswered questions.	Help Jose apply for grants and fellowships; encourage his (1) attendance and participation in local, regional, and national-level conferences; and (2) reading of professional materials.

(Continued)

(Continued)

	Student Behavior	Possible Action to Encourage Talent Development
11	Jose works with colleagues, a mentor, and alone to investigate, research, and problem solve in history.	Encourage and nurture Jose's research, writing, and presentation skills.
12	Jose realizes that history fulfills him; that history must be the focus of his life's work. His behaviors, life plans, and career will revolve around this discipline. He feels actualized by the knowledge and skills that he uses; he sees life in and through history.	Encourage Jose to publish his own work in professional journals and other related publications.

Adapted from *The Parallel Curriculum* (Tomlinson, et al., 2008) Figure 7.6.

WORKSHOP #42

Introductory Activities in the Curriculum of Identity Parallel

Session Objectives

The focus for each of the four elements (i.e., focusing questions, hook or teaser, rationale, performance standards) of introductory activities changes in the Curriculum of Identity.

- Focusing questions might address the role of the student within the discipline and elicit personal response.
- The hook or teaser may take on an introspective or personal focus.
- The rationale might include small group discussion around introspective questions.
- Performance standards will include those related to self-knowledge.

Masters

- Introductory Activity Suggestions for the Curriculum of Identity
- Sample Introductory Activities for the Curriculum of Identity

INTRODUCTORY ACTIVITY SUGGESTIONS FOR THE CURRICULUM OF IDENTITY

- Provide students with a graphic organizer of all fields within a discipline so that they can visualize the range of work done by practitioners within a discipline.
- Share with students an array of products that professionals in the discipline produce (e.g., in history: fiction and nonfiction books, newspaper articles, photographs, timelines, maps, videos, charts, journals, letters, and telegrams).

- Read aloud to students about famous and infamous people who have contributed to the field (e.g., *The Lighthouse Keeper's Daughter* by Arielle North Olsen; *Eleanor* by Barbara Cooney). Books that portray the famous people at the approximate age of the students are especially powerful.
- Introduce a timeline of important turning points in the discipline that includes the names and contributions of eminent people of both genders and a variety of cultures within the field. Seek students' answers to questions such as: *What did it take to become this person? What might he or she have been like as a ___ grader? In what ways am I like this famous person when he or she was my age? In what ways am I different? What parts of this person's work would interest me? What parts would I not enjoy?*
- Brainstorm personal characteristics of practicing professionals within the field both now and at earlier ages. Call on students to compare their own interests and abilities to those of practicing professionals.
- Share revealing audio clips, segments of documentaries, and newspaper articles about important moments and the people who shaped those moments.

Adapted from *The Parallel Curriculum* (Tomlinson, et al., 2008) Figure 7.4.

SAMPLE INTRODUCTORY ACTIVITIES FOR THE CURRICULUM OF IDENTITY

Focusing Questions

- Who are contemporary explorers?
- What were they like as students? How did they spend their time? What were their interests? How did they first become interested in geography, maps, navigation?
- How do they spend their time at work? On what sorts of questions and issues do they spend their time?
- In what ways do the interests and values of the contemporary explorers reflect or differ from your own?
- In what other ways are you like the contemporary explorers?
- In what other ways are you different from them?

Hook or Teaser

- The teacher plays a recording of Neil Armstrong's words as he walked on the moon's surface: "That's one small step for man; one giant leap for mankind."
- Then in small groups, students discuss answers to the prompt: What personal characteristics did Neil Armstrong possess that enabled him to take the first steps on the lunar surface in 1969? What similarities are there between Armstrong's characteristics and your own?

Rationale (Small Group Discussion Questions)

- What are the "frontiers" for your generation in the twenty-first century?
- If you became an explorer in the twenty-first century, what might your contribution or legacy be?
- In what ways are explorers important to you? To humankind?

Standards

- Students will develop an appreciation for the personal characteristics of explorers across time.
- Students will be able to compare their own personal qualities with those of explorers, past and present.

WORKSHOP #43

Teaching Strategies in the Curriculum of Identity Parallel

Session Objectives

While all types of teaching methods may be employed in a Curriculum of Identity, those that readily lend themselves to the acquisition of self-knowledge include methods that provide students with the opportunity to take on or otherwise closely examine the role of the practicing professional; and reflect on and construct self-knowledge as a result. Teaching strategies most appropriate for the Curriculum of Identity cluster toward the indirect end of the teaching strategies continuum.

Masters

- Teaching Activity Suggestions for the Curriculum of Identity

---

TEACHING ACTIVITY SUGGESTIONS FOR THE CURRICULUM OF IDENTITY

- Generate questions for students' written reflection and discussion throughout the unit to assist students in thinking about the knowledge that practitioners in the field use, problems they address, ways they work, personality traits, career development, personal and work goals, and so forth and what students can learn about themselves through examining these elements.
- Use independent investigations to provide students the opportunity to study research on, contributions of, and working modes in the discipline.
- Use shadowing experiences and mentorships to provide students with firsthand opportunities to learn about the day-to-day routines, values, and beliefs of professionals in the field.
- Use problem-based learning to enhance students' awareness of problem-solving abilities employed in the field.
- Use simulations to engage students in reflecting on the issues and problems of the discipline.
- Use visualization techniques to assist students in reflecting on past, current, and future selves.

Adapted from *The Parallel Curriculum* (Tomlinson, et al., 2008) Figure 7.4.

WORKSHOP #44

Learning Activities in the Curriculum of Identity Parallel

Session Overview

While it is important to embed a variety of thinking skills into learning activities, those learning activities that draw on executive processing skills and creative thinking are especially important for the goals and purposes of the Curriculum of Identity because of their capacity to promote student reflection and analysis. Students need to "feel" what it is like to be the practicing professional and gain a sense about what it means to be a historian, an anthropologist, a musician, a mathematician, an artist, or an environmental scientist, for example.

Masters

- Learning Activity Suggestions for the Curriculum of Identity
- Learning Task Example for the Curriculum of Identity

LEARNING ACTIVITY SUGGESTIONS FOR THE CURRICULUM OF IDENTITY

- Have students use a multiple-step process to identify, research, and plan to solve a problem in the discipline that requires a novel solution.
- Help students formulate discipline-related questions that they want to answer.
- Ask students to use appropriate criteria to select the best possible alternative in making decisions.
- Ask students to rank, prioritize, and sequence the steps involved in an independent investigation.
- Help students develop or refine the ability to set appropriate goals for their work, use these goals to guide their work, modify the goals at work progresses, and assess their work according to their goals.
- Help students develop the skills of introspection and the ability to compare and contrast their own personal characteristics and goals with those of the practicing professional.
- Use the driving questions of the parallel as journal prompts.

Adapted from *The Parallel Curriculum* (Tomlinson, et al., 2008) Figure 7.4.

LEARNING TASK EXAMPLE FOR THE CURRICULUM OF IDENTITY

Select a person from the accompanying list of men and women in science. In a presentation format of your choice, describe the contribution of your scientist and the impact of his or her legacy on the field. Highlight the challenges, setbacks, and successes that he or she faced in order to leave a legacy to the scientific world. Use at least five references, at least three of which must be primary source material (e.g., letters, photographs, personal correspondence, and audio- or videotapes).

As part of your presentation, or in a separate attachment, describe how you are like and unlike this person. How do you or might you handle the kinds of challenges, setbacks, and successes that this person faced. What legacy do *you* hope to leave the world?

WORKSHOP #45

Grouping Practices in the Curriculum of Identity Parallel

Session Overview

Teachers who work with a Curriculum of Identity will use many grouping patterns to help students see reflections of themselves within a discipline.

Masters

- Grouping Suggestions for the Curriculum of Identity

GROUPING SUGGESTIONS FOR THE CURRICULUM OF IDENTITY

- Use individual conferences to discuss student interests, reflection, growth in learning, and work profiles, and to forward student learning related to competencies in both content and personal reflection.
- Use small groups for (1) interest-based explorations related to the curriculum content, (2) analysis of the class learning and work profile, (3) debriefing activities, and (4) extension activities.
- Use pairs for think-alouds that support students' reflection and self-assessment, students' analyses of their learning and work profiles for emerging themes and patterns, and students' editing.
- Work with large groups of students to provide an overview of the unit, introduce the learning and work profile, hear guest speakers, and participate in field experiences.

Adapted from *The Parallel Curriculum* (Tomlinson, et al., 2008) Figure 7.4.

WORKSHOP #46

Resources in the Curriculum of Identity Parallel

Session Overview

Exemplary resources for the Curriculum of Identity are those that provide students with revealing glimpses into the personal lives and daily activities of practicing professionals. The critical task teachers face is to ensure alignment among the learning goals, the learning tasks, the resources, and students' unique learning needs (e.g., reading level, learning preferences, and interest areas).

Masters

- Resources Suggestions for the Curriculum of Identity

RESOURCES SUGGESTIONS
FOR THE CURRICULUM OF IDENTITY

- Locate schools and community members who are practicing professionals in careers related to the unit of study. Invite them to be guest speakers and mentors for students.
- Locate biographies, at appropriate reading levels, of historical and contemporary practicing professionals.
- Provide students with segments of audiotapes, documentaries, or newspaper articles that chronicle significant events in the lives of people who have contributed to the field.
- Provide students with a wide variety of products created by practicing professionals in the discipline. Provide time for students to examine the collection and ask questions.

Adapted from *The Parallel Curriculum* (Tomlinson, et al., 2008) Figure 7.4.

WORKSHOP #47

Products in the Curriculum of Identity Parallel

Session Overview

Products or performances should be chosen with care to:

- Align with the targeted learning goals, concepts, principles.
- Have the capacity to reveal the targeted knowledge or skill.
- Reflect the work of the practicing professional.
- Invite student reflection in ways that produce insights about personal traits, goals, preferences, values, and ways of working compared with those same traits in those who work in or are reflected in the discipline.

Students should be afforded regular opportunities to select the format for their products and self-assess their work to help them become aware of their place on the novice-to-expert continuum.

Masters

- Product Suggestions for the Curriculum of Identity

PRODUCT SUGGESTIONS FOR THE CURRICULUM OF IDENTITY

- Provide students with regular opportunities to analyze and reflect on products that reflect the work of practicing professionals.
- Encourage students to create portfolios of their best work samples. Provide opportunities for students to assess the growth reflected in the chronology of their portfolio pieces.
- Ensure that students have the opportunity for self-assessment using rubrics that have been designed for products and performances.
- Provide students with systematic opportunities to reflect on who they are becoming as learners and workers. Call on them to put their thoughts in journal entries, reflective essays, collages, tape-recorded reflections, and so on.

Adapted from *The Parallel Curriculum* (Tomlinson, et al., 2008) Figure 7.4.

WORKSHOP #48

Extensions in the Curriculum of Identity Parallel

Session Overview

Teachers can effectively use extension activities to increase a student's self-knowledge through exploration of key content. In this parallel, extension activities would likely include individual and small group investigations derived from the curriculum unit and students' interests. In a final reflection about a student's extension activity, a teacher needs to ask the student what new questions the student now has related to his or her interests, skills, values, goals, and so forth. A student's answer is an indication as to where he or she might need to go next in thinking and exploration.

Masters

• Extension Activity Suggestions for the Curriculum of Identity

---

EXTENSION ACTIVITY SUGGESTIONS
FOR THE CURRICULUM OF IDENTITY

- Provide opportunities for students to be involved with simulations related to the curriculum unit and their interests.
- Make available supplementary videotapes on related topics.
- Provide opportunities for students to visit in person or electronically with local experts and other professionals in related areas.
- Invite speakers to talk about cutting-edge research questions and state-of-the-art research techniques in their work and the discipline.
- Locate Webquests related to the curriculum topic and/or its practitioners.
- Find students a shadowing experience, internship, or mentorship when appropriate.
- Help students find community-based opportunities to investigate the work of practitioners in the discipline.
- Ask students to read journals or diaries, view videos, or interview professionals to learn about the lives and work of practitioners
- Ask students to read biographies and autobiographies or examine work samples or critiques of the work of experts in fields related to the unit's content goals and student interests.

Adapted from *The Parallel Curriculum* (Tomlinson, et al., 2008) Figure 7.4.

WORKSHOP #49

Differentiation and AID in the Curriculum of Identity Parallel

---

Session Overview

• By its very nature, the Curriculum of Identity is responsive to learner variance. Even with its flexible framework, though, there is a need for teachers to provide students with varying opportunities for continuous movement toward expertise within a field or discipline.

- At the heart of this parallel is a desire to help students think about themselves and their goals *in the context of the disciplines.*
- To respond to learner variance, students can reflect on themselves in relation to the topic they are studying instead of on the discipline in which it is housed. For example: students reflect on themselves as explorers *or* historians who study and write about the explorers; reflect on oneself as a biographer *or* reflect on oneself as a soldier, hero or pioneer.

Masters

- Differentiation and AID Suggestions for the Curriculum of Identity
- AID and the Curriculum of Identity Parallel

DIFFERENTIATION AND AID SUGGESTIONS FOR THE CURRICULUM OF IDENTITY

- Be aware that students are at different levels of development with respect to the content goals of the unit, interest in the discipline, and ability to be introspective.
- Provide support for students who may have potential in the field, but who have not yet displayed interest in the topic and/or discipline.
- Provide different levels of support to scaffold students' acquisition of content and skills related to their emerging sense of identity.
- Provide an array of materials to accommodate students' interests, prior experiences, reading abilities, and ability to draw inferences (e.g., in a mapping unit: copies of historical maps, star charts, maps of the ocean floor, town maps, road maps, topographical maps, relief maps, political maps, population maps, floor plans, treasure maps).
- Support increasing levels of student independence in self-assessment regarding goals.
- Assess students' current level of awareness of generic working skills, such as time management, ability to work in a team, leadership skills, responsibility, sociability, and so forth as they relate to practitioners in the discipline and to self.

Adapted from *The Parallel Curriculum* (Tomlinson, et al., 2008) Figure 7.4.

AID AND THE CURRICULUM OF IDENTITY PARALLEL

- Use longitudinal rubrics to help student and teacher locate and respond to a student's level of proficiency on a novice to expert continuum within a topic or discipline.
- Vary the resources (i.e., nonhuman and human) that students use. Nonhuman resources vary in reading difficulty, complexity, and/or the degree of inference required. Human resources vary as well because individuals have different levels of expertise within a field or domain as well as different ways of interacting with students.
- Increase the complexity of questions or problems with which students work and on which students reflect. Within each discipline are cutting-edge problems, questions, and issues. Students can begin their search for themselves in a curricular area by being involved at a "junior level." As they demonstrate increased interest and commitment to selected fields, they can take on increasingly more complex problems.

- Ask students to develop their own rubrics or scales to assess the proficiency of products in a topic or discipline that holds a special interest for them (e.g., a watercolor, a dance, an essay, a debate, a professional article, a science experiment, a map).
- Ask students to:
  - Look for and reflect on "truths," beliefs, ways of working, styles, and so on that typify the field.
  - Look for "roots" of theories, beliefs, and principles in a field and relating those theories, beliefs, and principles to the time when they "took root" in one's own life.
  - Look for and reflect on the meaning of paradoxes and contradictions in the discipline or field.
  - Engage in long-term problem solving on an intractable problem in the discipline that causes the student to encounter and mediate multiple points of view and reflect systematically on the experience.
  - Research and establish standards of quality work as defined by the discipline, applying those standards to the student's own work in the discipline over an extended time and reflecting systematically on the experience.
  - Collaborate with a high-level professional or practitioner in the field in shared problem solving and reflection.
  - Challenge or look for limitations of the ideas, models, ways of working, or belief systems of the discipline.
  - Look for parallels (or contrasts) in personal prejudices, blind spots, assumptions, habits, and those evident in the field.
  - Study and reflect on one discipline by using the concepts, principles, and modes of working of another discipline, reflecting on the interactions and insights gained.

Adapted from *The Parallel Curriculum* (Tomlinson, et al., 2008) Figure 7.9.

WORKSHOP #50

Closure in the Curriculum of Identity Parallel

Session Overview

Closure activities in a Curriculum of Identity unit ensure that students reflect on important concepts and principles of the discipline, as well as what students are coming to understand about themselves as learners and people with contributions to make to their world as they study a topic, discipline, and practitioners in the discipline.

Masters

- Closure Suggestions for the Curriculum of Identity

CLOSURE SUGGESTIONS FOR THE CURRICULUM OF IDENTITY

- Use the focusing questions for the Identity Parallel to guide closure activities.
- Ask students to summarize, explain, and provide supporting evidence for key concepts and principles in the content they are studying.

- Guide students in reflecting on the range of contributors and contributions to the field.
- Have students analyze the work of experts in the discipline according to ways of working, work settings and conditions, habits of mind, issues and problems dealt with, methods used, ethical issues, and contributions to society.
- Have students compare attributes of individuals who have impacted the field (or society through the field) positively and negatively and reflect on personal insights about the similarities and differences.
- Use two-column journals, comparison/contrast organizers, classroom data charts, and similar data-gathering and analysis formats to have students reflect on what their study of the discipline, its methods, and its disciplinarians are teaching them about themselves individually and as a group.

Adapted from *The Parallel Curriculum* (Tomlinson, et al., 2008) Figure 7.4.

6

Combining the Parallels

Note to Facilitator

This chapter reverts to the format of Chapters 1 through 3. To prepare for this workshop, you may wish to review Chapter 3, "Using the Four Parallel Curricula as a Comprehensive Curriculum Model: Philosophy and Pragmatism," in *The Parallel Curriculum in the Classroom Book 1: Essays for Application Across the Content Areas, K–12* (Tomlinson, et al., 2005).

WORKSHOP #51

Using Multiple Parallels

Session Overview

This last series of workshops focuses on flexible options for using the Parallel Curriculum Model (PCM). It is possible to write a unit to match any one of the parallels, but it is also possible to build aspects of more than one, or even all four parallels, into a single unit.

Masters

- Why Use Multiple Parallels in a Unit?
- Parallels as Support for Thematic Study
- Parallels to Build From a Common Foundation

Session Details

Introduction

As a review, use the matching game (see Appendix B) to reinforce the components of curriculum that participants will want to consider when combining parallels. Note any difficulties participants are having and review as needed.

Teaching and Learning Activities

Say: "Up to this point, we have examined each of the four parallels in isolation to help you become comfortable with the "flavor" of each one. In these final sessions, we will focus on using the parallels in combination. As you worked with your unit, you might have found that although you were focusing your learning on a specific parallel, in some instances another parallel might better suit your needs and/or those of your particular students." (Ask participants to share any such experiences or insights.)

Say: "The authors of the *The Parallel Curriculum* (Tomlinson, et al., 2008) encourage you think about ways to combine parallels or use aspects of one parallel to enhance a unit based on another when it seems appropriate to do so. It is possible to use a flexible approach to designing curriculum with the parallels because all of them are rooted in a conceptual understanding of a topic and/or discipline (the Core Curriculum)."

- Share: "Why Use Multiple Parallels in a Unit?"

Say: "There are many possible configurations and uses of the various parallels to guide a broad range of learners in continual growth toward expertise in a discipline. We will examine two ways in this session and three additional ways in the next to think about combining parallels in the next session."

- One way to combine parallels is to use them as support for thematic study, an approach to helping students grasp the interconnectedness of knowledge. Students would focus on a specific theme or themes and use multiple topics to explore the theme(s). See "The Parallels as Support for Thematic Study" to illustrate this option.
- A second way to combine parallels is to choose one parallel as the foundation parallel and then use the parallels to enhance, extend, or reinforce important ideas and skills of the unit at specific points in the unit. It is possible for any of the parallels to serve as the foundation parallel for a unit and for any or all of the other parallels to diversify and extend the unit. (Remember, that in a sense, the Core Curriculum serves as a foundation for the other parallels.) Share "Parallels to Build From a Common Foundation."
- Ask participants to choose one of the methods for combing parallels described so far and use that method to sketch out a general or rough plan for a unit that combines parallels.

Closure/Looking Forward

Ask participants to share their ideas with a colleague or group of colleagues. If you have time, go on to Workshop #52. If not, tell the group that in the next session they will examine three other ways to use the parallels in combination.

WHY USE MULTIPLE PARALLELS IN A UNIT?

Advantages to Using More Than One Parallel
- Gives students multiple perspectives on the same content.
- Reaches more students because of the capacity of such units to tap into a range of interest areas.
- Provides reinforcing learning experiences that enhance students' capacity to retain, retrieve, and use the content they study.

PARALLELS AS SUPPORT FOR THEMATIC STUDY

Grade Four: The Study of Change

Teachers use each parallel to help students investigate "change." The parallels are of equal importance in this example:

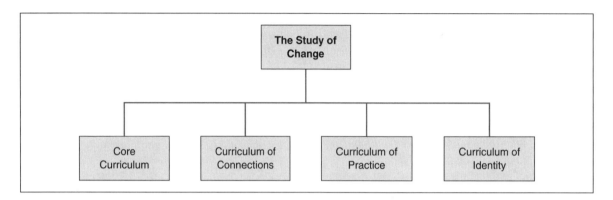

Aspects of change students will explore during one quarter or trimester:

Discipline	*Theme Related to Change*
Science	Weather
Social Studies	Westward expansion
Language Arts	Biography and autobiography
Math	Move from one operation to another
Music	Change of keys and rhythm

Example adapted from *The Parallel Curriculum* (Tomlinson, et al., 2002) pp. 252–253.

Lesson activities suited to each parallel:

Core Curriculum Parallel	• Define change. • Identify key principles related to change. • Introduce key skills needed to work in each discipline area specified by standards document and textbook.
Curriculum of Connections Parallel	• Conduct periodic lessons in which students compare and contrast the concept of change in the various content areas they are studying.
Curriculum of Practice Parallel	• Ask students to use the methods of a practitioner in one of the disciplines to observe and report on a significant change currently taking place in that discipline.
Curriculum of Identity Parallel	• Ask students to do an illustrated autobiographical sketch in which they compare their own interests and perspectives to those of an expert in one of the disciplines they have studied.

PARALLELS TO BUILD FROM A COMMON FOUNDATION

Subject: Art

In this example, the foundation parallel is the Curriculum of Practice. The Core Curriculum, the Curriculum of Connections, and the Curriculum of Identity receive varying amounts of emphasis.

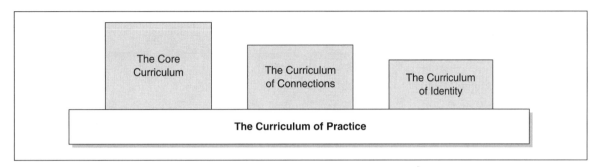

Unit Activities

Curriculum of Practice Parallel	• Teacher works with students to orient them to the nature of graphic design as an expert sees it, methods of graphic designers, problem identification and solution strategies, and so on. • Teacher asks students to work as graphic designers to identify and solve a graphic design problem in an interest area such as theater, music, medicine, or sports.
Core Curriculum Parallel	• The teacher includes a series of lessons to help students identify key concepts and methodologies of graphic design in the work of contemporary graphic artists.
Curriculum of Connections Parallel	• The teacher shows students examples of graphic design from a range of periods and cultures and asks students to use their knowledge of the concepts and methods of design, as well as of technology and culture, to hypothesize the period and culture that the designs represent.
Curriculum of Identity Parallel	• Students select a graphic design from a broad array of options and discuss ways in which both the design and design process used in creating their selections is metaphorical for them as people and artists.

Adapted from *The Parallel Curriculum* (Tomlinson, et al., 2002) pp. 253–254.

WORKSHOP #52

More Ways to Use Multiple Parallels

Session Overview

This workshop provides participants with additional ways to think about using a combination of parallels within one unit of study.

(Continued)

(Continued)

Masters

- A Layered Approach to Using the Parallels
- Using the Parallels for Varied Purposes Within a Single Unit
- Designing Individual Learning Pathways Using the Parallel Curriculum Model

Session Details

Introduction

If needed, review "Why Use Multiple Parallels in a Unit" from Workshop #51.

Teaching and Learning Activities

Say: "In our last session, we looked at two possibilities for combing parallels: using a thematic approach to combine parallels and using one parallel as a foundation for work in the other parallels. Another way to combine parallels is to use a layered approach in which work in one parallel leads to work in another, followed by another, and so on. See "A Layered Approach to Using the Parallels" to illustrate this option.

- Parallels may also be used for a variety of purposes at a variety of points in a unit. See "Using the Parallels for Varied Purposes Within a Single Unit" for four possible scenarios.
- When teachers have one or more students who have advanced knowledge, understanding, and skill with regard to a unit of study, the parallels may be used as a roadmap for substitute or more complex work. See "Designing Individual Learning Pathways Using the Parallel Curriculum Model" for an illustration.
- Ask participants to choose one of the options described in this session and use that method to sketch out a general or rough plan for a unit that combines parallels. If possible, provide time for participants to more fully flesh out either this plan or the one they sketched out in workshop 51.

Closure/Looking Forward

Ask participants to share their ideas with a colleague or group of colleagues.

A LAYERED APPROACH TO USING THE PARALLELS

Discipline/Level: History/High School

Topic: Causes and Effects of the American Revolution

The teacher plans lessons to follow a sequence of learning that makes use of each parallel in turn as students progress throughout a unit of study. Although this example has a layer for each parallel, another teacher might choose to only use two or three layers.

Core Curriculum Parallel

- Introduce fundamental facts about the time period.
- Introduce concepts of *conflict, conflict resolution, revolution,* and *cause and effect.*
- Introduce skills of comparing and contrasting, document analysis, providing credible evidence for positions.

↓

Curriculum of Connections Parallel

- Use a range of documents to analyze causes and effects of revolutions in art, politics, and technology—comparing causes and effects of those revolutions to causes and effects of the American Revolution.

↓

Curriculum of Identity Parallel

- Simulate a conflict resolution scenario.
- Examine their own processes and abilities as arbiters.
- Predict roles and issues that will occur for those seeking to resolve conflicts between England and the colonists during the American Revolution.

↓

Curriculum of Practice Parallel

- Work in groups to analyze primary and secondary documents related to the end of the American Revolution.
- Find common themes that illustrate how the period was shaped by conflict and conflict resolution.
- Present findings in a class symposium during which each group will both present their findings and respond to findings of other groups in the role of historian.

Adapted from *The Parallel Curriculum* (Tomlinson, et al., 2002) pp. 254–255.

USING THE PARALLELS FOR VARIED PURPOSES WITHIN A SINGLE UNIT

Discipline: Language Arts

Novel Unit: To Kill a Mockingbird

Below are four different ways teachers might use one or more of the parallels to enhance a specific unit. One teacher might use just one set of ideas to enhance a unit, another might use several of these ideas at various points in a unit of study.

Curriculum of Connections

- The teacher forms interest-based groups to examine ways in which the concepts of justice and injustice currently relate to race, gender, handicapping condition, and/or age in the areas of medical care, housing, education, or sports.
- As students work together, they formulate a sense of the complexity of the concepts themselves as well as ways in which people's perspectives affect their views about justice and injustice.
- The teacher has captured the interest of students and has begun to build a bridge between their own world and a pair of abstract concepts.

Curriculum of Connections as Introduction

To Kill a Mockingbird Unit

Core Curriculum

- Lead the class in developing several assertions or hypotheses about that relationship (e.g., "A person's position of power in a group affects that person's perspective on justice").
- Examine the novel for confirming or refuting evidence of the assertions.
- Ask students to diagram or map the relationship between power and justice/injustice.
- Lead students to develop a set of principles about the relationship between power and justice/injustice that they believe they can support.

Core Curriculum to deepen understanding of unit concepts

Curriculum of Identity

- Students select a character from the novel with whom they most identify and write an interior monologue from this character's perspective.
- Students do the same kind of writing from the perspective of a character with whom they find it most difficult to identify.
- Students read *Composing a Life* by Mary Catherine Bateson (1989) and then reflect on what the novel and interior monologues show them about how they are composing their own lives.

Curriculum of Identity to forge new understandings

To Kill a Mockingbird Unit

Curriculum of Practice

- First, introduce the research method of ethnography, teaching its basic purposes, principles, and methods; examine excerpts from published ethnographies, ethnographers' notes, and ethnographers' reflections on analyzing their data.
- As a culminating product, students play the role of ethnographer.
  - **Goal** Create a brief piece of ethnographic writing that evokes an authentic and informed sense of place, time, character, and significance reminiscent of author's work.
  - **Goal** Review key elements of fiction and use them with the keen eye and ear of a good writer.
  - **Rubric** Provides guidance.

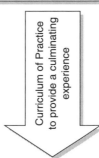

Curriculum of Practice to provide a culminating experience

To Kill a Mockingbird Unit

Adapted from *The Parallel Curriculum* (Tomlinson, et al., 2002) pp. 256–257.

DESIGNING INDIVIDUAL LEARNING PATHWAYS USING THE PARALLEL CURRICULUM MODEL

Environmental Science

This is a unit plan designed to make the curriclum a better fit for a highly advanced student. The detours respond to the students' interests, learning preferences, and specific talents. Although this example plans detours in all the parallels, other students may need a detour in just one, two, or three of the parallels. You might think about these detours in three ways:

Add to the curriculum means that a parallel will become an addendum to some feature of the preexisting lesson.

Replace and integrate the curriculum means that a parallel becomes a substitute for a feature of the lesson that already has been learned or is not appropriate for learners who may already have mastered portions of the curriculum.

Extend the curriculum means that a parallel is used to elaborate a feature of the preexisting lesson.

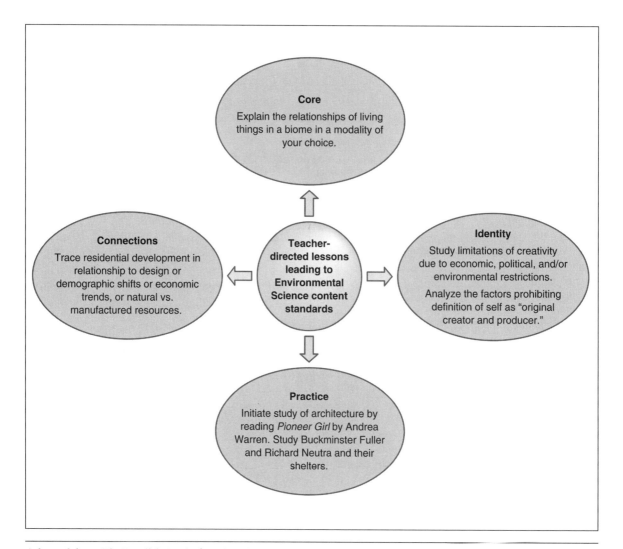

Adapted from *The Parallel Curriculum* (Tomlinson, et al., 2002) Figure 8.5.

WORKSHOP #53

Using the Parallel Curriculum Model

Session Overview

In this final workshop, participants will revisit key factors for shaping curriculum using the PCM. They also will be reminded of how and why it is important to stay true to the intent and purposes of the parallels when designing curriculum via this model. A self-assessment feedback tool is also included in this session.

Masters

- Making Decisions About the Use of the Parallel Curriculum Model
- Ensuring Fidelity to the Parallel Curriculum Model
- "A Final Thought"
- Self-Reflection

Session Details

Introduction

Say: "This session provides an overview of some key factors that should shape the decisions we make about curriculum. What new ways of thinking about curriculum design have you gained from these workshops?

Teaching and Learning Activities

- Share the overhead "Making Decisions About the Use of the Parallel Curriculum Model."
- Introduce key factors that should shape decisions about curriculum.

Say: "The PCM has great potential to enhance teaching and learning in many settings. The authors of the model know, however, that this model will not always be the best approach for all students and teachers, in all contexts, with all learning goals. They do understand also that when it *does* provide a fruitful way to think about curriculum design, it is should be viewed as more a description of a rich curriculum than a rigid template for curriculum design. The PCM thus calls for flexible application to ensure a match between learning goals, students, teachers, context, and decisions about how to arrange the curriculum."

Say: "No matter how we implement the PCM or individual parallels within the model, it is vital that we stay true to the intents and purposes of the model as a whole and to the intents and purposes of each parallel."

- Share "Ensuring Fidelity to the Parallel Curriculum Model."

Closure

- This is the final session in the seminar. Copy and distribute the "Self-Reflection" sheet for participants to complete. (You might consider giving this sheet—or a part of this sheet—out at the end of every chapter or part way through the entire series of workshops so that you can use this information to better match participants needs along the way.)

(Continued)

(Continued)

- After participants have completed "Self-Reflection," invite them to share any responses they recorded with the whole group. Or allow participants time to work alone or in small groups to take notes or immediately apply what they gleaned from the reflective discussion and/or the "Self-Reflection" sheet.
- Adapt and/or abbreviate the suggested closing comments below to suit your presentation style.

Say: "I hope that this seminar series about the Parallel Curriculum Model has been both a challenge and an encouragement to you as you do the hard work of developing curriculum that reshapes you—the teacher—even as it reshapes the world of students. In the end, teachers construct knowledge as their students do—by seeking meaning, making connections, putting ideas to work at a high level of professional quality, and reflecting on what their work teaches them about themselves—even as it teaches the young people they serve."

MAKING DECISIONS ABOUT THE USE OF THE PARALLEL CURRICULUM MODEL

The Nature of Learning Goals

Considering the learning goals, concepts, and principles will help a teacher understand which portions of the PCM would be most effective in developing a particular segment of curriculum.

The Nature of the Students

Curriculum plans should be made with full awareness of the students whom the curriculum is designed to teach. Things to consider include developmental level of students, span of student readiness, student interests, best match between students and PCM parallel(s), and so on.

The Nature of the Teacher

It is also critical to ask whether the curriculum is a good match for the teacher(s) who will teach it. A rich and challenging curriculum can encourage teacher growth, just as it can support student growth. But if the curriculum plan is "too far ahead" of a teacher's current knowledge and skills, results for both teacher and students are likely to be poor.

The Context of the Curriculum

Curriculum on paper differs from the reality that is constrained by such elements as time, materials, space, and so forth. So, it is important to consider the real-world context and address issues such as time allotment, available books and materials, support of colleagues, community resources, learning space, and appropriate match of the PCM.

Other Teaching Considerations

Beyond, and related to, knowledge of goals, students, teacher, and context, there are still many decisions to be made about how to teach the curriculum using any particular model.

ENSURING FIDELITY TO THE PARALLEL CURRICULUM MODEL

Nonnegotiables

When we write units using the PCM, we must be sure of the following:

- Units must be focused on concepts and principles.
- Units must require students to regularly seek and pose answers to a parallel's driving questions.
- The "intent" of the parallel must be at the forefront of all components of the curriculum (i.e., introductory activities, teaching strategies, learning activities, products, resources, closure)
- The unit must provide opportunities for Ascending Intellectual Demand so that all students work in increasingly expertlike ways

A FINAL THOUGHT

The PCM is rooted in the beliefs that all learners must construct meaning from what they study and that learning becomes more engaging, relevant, durable, transferable, and purposeful as students understand the key concepts, principles, and skills of the disciplines; come to see those concepts and principles as the connective tissue that binds the universe of knowledge; apply the understandings and skills in ways that empower them as thinkers and producers of knowledge; and see the disciplines as a way to understand themselves both now and in the future. (Tomlinson, et al., 2002, p. 264)

SELF-REFLECTION

1. As a result of this training, what have I learned that is most relevant to me?
2. What will I use immediately that I have received in this training?
3. What, if anything, did I hope to learn but did not?
4. Would I recommend PCM to a colleague? Why or why not?
5. Which parallel, if any, resonated with me most? Explain.
6. This seminar validated what I already do when I . . .
7. The next steps I see that need to happen for me to continue my work with the PCM are . . .
8. The support I need from my colleagues and/or administrator so that I can continue to work with the PCM and share my enthusiasm and teachings with others are . . .

Appendixes

APPENDIX A

Facilitation Suggestions

Each workshop session in this guide includes masters designed to help educators understand key aspects of the Parallel Curriculum Model and its individual parallels. This material highlights the intent, purpose, benefits, and/or driving questions of each parallel. It serves to provide key information of each parallel so that participants become knowledgeable enough to design or redesign their own curriculum to be in alignment with the parallels. To allow for interaction with the material presented and to help participants assimilate it, here are several suggestions that you can use throughout the series of workshops.

1. Questioning

Pose questions to teachers throughout all sessions to help foster critical and creative thinking. Here are some you might consider.

- To what extent do you agree with this approach or these approaches to curriculum design?
- Can you think of additional approaches or parallels that might be useful?
- Why would a teacher want or need such a framework?
- How can your current curriculum be better served by this parallel?
- How does this bullet (on the master) address the needs of students?
- What are specific examples in your classroom that speak to a particular bullet?
- What are the advantages to organizing curriculum in this way? Why don't we do this more often?
- Using the master that includes the driving questions, consider how each question could assist practitioners in helping them craft lessons. How might student learning look different using these questions as a guide?
- Select any unit of study. How might the content be explored using each of the parallels?
- How does this type of curriculum design compare to the curriculum you have in place at the state, district, or school level?
- Compare and contrast the curriculum you currently use in your classroom with the curriculum designed according to a specific parallel. Discuss the strengths and weaknesses of findings.

- Contrast the goals of one parallel with the goals of another. In what ways are they similar? In what ways are they different?
- Compare and contrast a particular unit in one parallel with a unit designed using another parallel.

2. Curriculum Components

As you discuss and review the components that will serve as the template for curriculum design for each parallel, consider these discussion prompts. Many are geared specifically to a particular component, but use them also as a guide to craft your own questions and generate teaching ideas for other components.

- Discuss how a concept map would look in one parallel versus another parallel. For example, how would a concept map look in a Curriculum of Connections unit when compared to a concept map in a Core Curriculum unit?
- How do introductory activities within a Core Curriculum unit compare to introductory activities from an Identity unit?
- How are learning activities different from teaching strategies?
- Make a list of the teaching strategies that are most familiar to you. Identify ones that are less familiar. Conduct a sharing of best practices in which you have participants share classroom experiences with the teaching strategies that are familiar to them.
- What does it mean when a learning activity is *hands-on*?
- Ask teachers to share the kinds of products they assign in their classrooms. Create a list of these products. Are these products different than the ones typically offered to students? Have teachers share success stories of certain product options to further entice teachers reluctant to offer more options to do so. (For fun, suggest they design a commercial to convince a group of colleagues to "purchase" a particular type of product for use in their classroom.)
- Make a list of the teaching methods that would work in tandem with the tenets of each particular parallel.
- Make a list of the products that would be most in alignment with each of the parallels.
- How would you provide increasing levels of challenge within a given unit in each parallel?
- What specialized resources would push forward student learning in a given parallel?

3. Teaching Strategies

Your teaching style will dictate how you use the following suggestions for teaching the material.

- Take key questions specific to the material you are presenting and write one question per note card. As you present an overhead or handout, have each participant select one note card from a hat or box then find a partner. Have participants turn to the person seated next to them and read their questions and discuss answers. When pairs are finished discussing each of the two questions, invite them to share with the whole group. Promote further discussion with those questions that need additional probing. *Variation:* Instead of having participants turn to their neighbors to partner up and discuss answers to each of their questions, have participants walk around the room and find a partner they barely know or have not yet met. When they pair up, have pairs discuss each person's questions and discuss possible answers. Pairs are then seated. Springboard whole group discussion by asking volunteers to share their questions and answers.

• See "Matching Game" (Appendix B). It is designed as a check for understanding. You can adapt this technique for use at any point throughout the staff development sessions. You might even play the game at the first session to preassess participants and again as a postassessment.

• Synectics is a teaching method in which teachers and students share or develop metaphors, similes, and/or analogies that build a bridge between students' prior knowledge or experience and new learning. It is one of the teaching methods discussed in Workshop #7. Use synectics as a teaching method yourself when leading participants to understand selected material presented. For example, the Curriculum of Connection Parallel can be viewed as a *bridge* that links time periods, disciplines, cultures, and locations. Or ask "How is the _____ (e.g., Curriculum of Connections) _____ like ___ (e.g., a swing set) _____."

APPENDIX B

Matching Game

Game Overview

Use this game as a preassessment, mid-unit check, and/or final review. In this game, participants match terms and definitions. The term cards represent the four parallels and the ten components. Participants can either walk around the room and read a card to each person until a matching definition is found. Or, you can make a set of terms and definitions for pairs or trios to match while seated at a table. For some terms, there is more than one definition.

Version A: Each Participant Chooses a Card and Walks Around to Find a Match

Preparing for the Game

1. Copy the terms and definitions on heavy bond paper. Use the same color for all cards.

2. Using a cutting board, cut on the dotted lines to make cards.

3. Put all of the cards in a box or hat.

Playing the Game

1. Instruct participants to choose one card from the box or hat. Depending on the size of your group, some participants might select more than one card.

2. Tell participants to walk around the room and read each other the cards they are holding.

3. When participants find a match with the key component and a definition or definitions, they are to go to a designated part of the room. Note there is more than one definition for some terms.

4. After all participants are grouped appropriately with a key term and definition(s), they read their cards to the whole group.

5. Everyone listens to the reading of cards to determine if the matches are indeed correct.

Version B: Small Group Matching Terms to Definitions

Preparing for the Game

1. Copy the terms and definitions on heavy bond paper. Use one color for the terms and *another color* for the definitions so it is easy to distinguish between the two groups.

2. Using a cutting board, cut on the dotted lines to make cards.

3. Put each set of cards in an envelope—terms and definitions.

Playing the Game

1. Instruct small groups to lay out all the cards in the envelope and match terms with definitions.

2. After each group has finished, give them "Answers to Game Cards" so they check their own matches.

TERMS

content/ standards	resources	introductory activities
assessments	differentiation based on learner need	core curriculum parallel
products	extension activities	grouping strategies
teaching strategies	curriculum of connections parallel	curriculum of practice parallel
learning activities	curriculum of identity parallel	ascending intellectual demand

DEFINITIONS

represents daily or short-term student learning or provides longer-term culminating evidence of student knowledge and understanding	varied tools and techniques teachers use to determine the extent to which students have mastery of learning goals	materials that support learning during the teaching and learning activities
set the stage for a unit	pre-planned or serendipitous experiences that emerge from learning goals and students' interests	what we want students to know, understand, and do
optimizing the match between the curriculum and students' unique learning needs	a kind of differentiation devoted to escalating student expertise	lecture, drill and recitation, simulation, role playing
predicting, summarizing, problem solving, classifying	cognitive experiences that help students perceive, process, rehearse, store, and transfer knowledge, understanding, and skills	curriculum that establishes a rich framework of knowledge, understanding and skills most relevant to a discipline
varied approaches used to arrange students for effective learning in the classroom	helps students encounter and interact with the key concepts, principles, and skills in a variety of settings, times, and circumstances	methods teachers use to model, coach, guide, or transfer in the classroom

helps students see themselves in relation to the discipline both now and with possibilities for the future	methods teachers use to introduce, explain, or demonstrate in the classroom	broad statements about what grade-level students should know and be able to do
might include a "hook" or "teaser" to motivate students	performances or work samples created by students that provide evidence of student learning	helps students function with increasing skill and confidence in a discipline as professionals would function

Answers for Game Cards

Component	Definition
Content/Standard	What we want students to know, understand, and do
	Broad statements about what grade-level students should know and be able to do
	Often written as objectives, grade-level expectations, or as broad K–12 standards statements
Assessments	Varied tools and techniques teachers use to determine the extent to which students have mastery of learning goals
	Data gathered before, during, and after instruction that serves to inform subsequent teaching and learning
Introductory Activities	Might include a "hook" or "teaser" to motivate students
	Sets the stage for a unit
Teaching Strategies	Methods teachers use to introduce, explain, or demonstrate in the classroom
	Methods teachers use to model, coach, guide, or transfer in the classroom
	Lecture, drill and recitation, simulation, role playing, and so on

(Continued)

(Continued)

Component	Definition
Learning Activities	Cognitive experiences that help students perceive, process, rehearse, store, and transfer knowledge, understanding, and skills
	Predicting, summarizing, problem solving, and classifying
Grouping Strategies	Varied approaches used to arrange students for effective learning in the classroom
Products	Performances or work samples created by students that provide evidence of student learning
	Represents daily or short-term student learning or provides longer-term culminating evidence of student knowledge and understanding
Resources	Materials that support learning during the teaching and learning activities
Extension Activities	Preplanned or serendipitous experiences that emerge from learning goals and students' interests
Differentiation Based on Learner Need	Optimizing the match between the curriculum and students' unique learning needs
Ascending Intellectual Demand	A kind of differentiation devoted to escalating student expertise
Core Curriculum Parallel	Curriculum that establishes a rich framework of the knowledge, understanding, and skills most relevant to a discipline
Curriculum of Connections	Helps students encounter and interact with the key concepts, principles, and skills in a variety of settings, times, and circumstances
Curriculum of Practice	Helps students function with increasing skill and confidence in a discipline as professionals would function
Curriculum of Identity	Helps students see themselves in relation to the discipline both now and with possibilities for the future

APPENDIX C

Key Attributes of the Parallel Curriculum Model

As you proceed from one workshop to the next, it is imperative that participants are clear about four essential attributes of the model (see below). Reinforce these attributes whenever possible.

Concepts and Principles

What should always be evident to students and continuously revisited is that the Parallel Curriculum is concept-based and principle-driven. Ask: *How do these lessons help students see the concepts and principles?*

Key Components

Individual components of a curriculum unit (e.g., content, introductory activities, products) should always reflect the parallel for which the unit is designed. Ask: *Do the key components reflect the concepts, principles, and the essence of the particular parallel?*

Driving Questions

There is a set of questions for each parallel that help focus students on the key intent or deep meaning of each parallel. Ask: *Which driving questions does the unit ask students to answer?*

Ascending Intellectual Demand (AID)

As students become more advanced in their knowledge, understanding, and skill in a domain, the challenge level of materials and tasks will need to increase. AID is the escalating match between the learner and the curriculum so that all learners move along a curriculum toward expertise in one or more disciplinary areas. To apply AID is to guide all learners to walk increasingly in the paths of experts. Teachers need to extend the curriculum in ways that provide growth for learners to chart a course toward ever-increasing proficiency. Ask: *As you redesign lessons for each parallel, have you accounted for AID so even the most advanced learners have the opportunity to move on an upward continuum toward expertise?*

APPENDIX D

Driving Questions of the Parallel Curriculum Model

Driving Questions of the Core Curriculum

- What does this information mean?
- Why does this information matter?
- How is the information organized to help people use it better?
- Why do these ideas make sense?
- How do these ideas make sense?
- What are these ideas and skills for?
- How do these ideas and skills work?
- How can I use these ideas and skills?

Adapted from *The Parallel Curriculum* (Tomlinson, et al., 2008) Figure 4.1.

Driving Questions of the Curriculum of Connections

- What key concepts and principles have I learned?
- In what other contexts can I use what I have learned?
- How do the ideas and skills I have learned work in other contexts?
- How do I use the ideas and skills to develop insights or solve problems?
- How do different settings cause me to change or reinforce my earlier understandings?
- How do I adjust my way of thinking and working when I encounter new contexts?
- How do I know if my adjustments are effective?
- How does looking at one thing help me understand another?
- Why do different people have different perspectives on the same issue?
- How are perspectives shaped by time, place, culture, events, and circumstances?
- In what ways is it beneficial for me to examine varied perspectives on a problem or issue?
- How do I assess the relative strengths and weaknesses of differing viewpoints?
- What connections do I see between what I am studying and my own life and times?

Adapted from *The Parallel Curriculum* (Tomlinson, et al., 2008) Figure 5.2.

Driving Questions of the Curriculum of Practice

- How do practitioner-scholars organize knowledge and skills in this discipline?
- How do practitioners use the discipline's concepts and principles in daily practice?
- What are the routine problems in the discipline?
- What strategies does a practitioner use to solve routine and nonroutine problems in the discipline?
- How does the practitioner know which skills to use under given circumstances?
- How does a practitioner sense when approaches and methods are ineffective in a given instance?
- What are the methods used by practitioners and contributors in the field to generate new questions, new knowledge, and solve problems?
- What are indicators of quality and success in the discipline?

Adapted from The Parallel Curriculum (Tomlinson, et al., 2008) Figure 6.1.

Driving Questions of the Curriculum of Identity

- What do practitioners and contributors in the discipline think about?
- To what degree is this familiar, surprising, and/or intriguing to me?
- When I am intrigued by an idea, what do I gain from that, give as a result of that, and what difference does it make?
- How do people in this discipline think and work?
- In what ways do those processes seem familiar, surprising, and/or intriguing to me?
- What are the problems and issues on which practitioners and contributors in this discipline spend their lives?
- To what degree are those intriguing to me?
- What is the range of vocational and avocational possibilities in this discipline?
- In which ones can I see myself working?
- What difficulties do practitioners and contributors in this discipline encounter?
- How have they coped with the difficulties?
- How do I think I would cope with them?
- What are the ethical principles at the core of the discipline?
- How are those like and unlike my ethics?
- Who have been the "heroes" of the evolving discipline?
- What are the attributes of the "heroes?"
- What do I learn about myself by studying them?
- Who have been the "villains" of the evolving discipline?
- What are the attributes of the "villains"?
- What do I learn about myself by studying about them?
- How do people in this discipline handle ambiguity, uncertainty, persistence, failure, success, collaboration, and compromise?
- How do I handle those things?
- What is the wisdom this discipline has contributed to the world?
- How has that affected me?
- To what degree can I see myself contributing to that wisdom?
- How might I shape the discipline over time?
- How might it shape me?

Adapted from *The Parallel Curriculum* (Tomlinson, et al., 2008) Figure 7.3.

APPENDIX E

The Parallel Curriculum: A Model for Curriculum Planning (Reference Sheet)

The Core or Basic Curriculum	The Curriculum of Connections	The Curriculum of Practice	The Curriculum of Identity
The Core Curriculum is the foundational curriculum that establishes a rich framework of knowledge, understanding, and skills most relevant to the discipline. It is inclusive of and extends state and district expectations. It is the starting point or root system for all of the parallels in this model.	This curriculum is derived from and extends the Core Curriculum. It is designed to help students encounter and interact with the key concepts, principles, and skills in a variety of settings, times, and circumstances.	This curriculum is derived from and extends the Core Curriculum. Its purpose is to help students function with increasing skill and confidence in a discipline as professionals would function. It exists for the purpose of promoting students' expertise as practitioners of the discipline.	This curriculum is derived from and extends the Core Curriculum. It is designed to help students see themselves in relation to the discipline both now and with possibilities for the future; understand the discipline more fully by connecting it with their lives and experiences; increase awareness of their preferences, strengths, interests, and need for growth; and think about themselves as stewards of the discipline who may contribute to it and/or through it. The Curriculum of Identity uses curriculum as a catalyst for self-definition and self-understanding, with the belief that by looking outward to the discipline, students can find a means of looking inward.
The Core or Basic Curriculum:	The Curriculum of Connections is designed to help students think about and apply key concepts, principles, and skills:	The Curriculum of Practice asks students to:	The Curriculum of Identity asks students to:
• Is built on key facts, concepts, principles, and skills essential to discipline.	• In a range of instances throughout the discipline.	• Understand the nature of the discipline in a real-world application manner.	• Reflect on their skills and interests as they relate to the discipline.
• Is coherent in its organization.	• Across disciplines.	• Define and assume a role as a means of studying the discipline.	• Understand ways in which their interests might be useful to the discipline and ways in which the discipline might serve as a means for helping them develop their skills and interests.
• Is purposefully focused and organized to achieve essential outcomes.	• Across time and time periods.	• Understand the impact of this discipline on other disciplines and other disciplines on this discipline.	
• Promotes understanding rather than rote learning.	• Across locations.		
• Is taught in a meaningful context.	• Across cultures.	• Become a disciplinary problem solver rather than being a problem solver using the subject matter of the discipline.	
• Causes students to grapple with ideas and questions, using both critical and creative thinking.	• Across times, locations, and cultures.		
• Is mentally and affectively engaging and satisfying to learners.	• Through varied perspectives.	• Understand and use the discipline as a means of looking at and making sense of the world.	
• Results in evidence of worthwhile student production.	• As impacted by various conditions (social, economic, technological political, etc.)	• Develop a means of escaping the rut of certainty about knowledge.	
	• Through the eyes of various people who affected and are affected by the ideas.		
	• By examining links between concepts and development of the disciplines.		

The Core or Basic Curriculum	The Curriculum of Connections	The Curriculum of Practice	The Curriculum of Identity
		• Comprehend the daily lives of workers or professionals in the discipline: working conditions, hierarchical structures, fiscal aspects of the work, peer, or collegial dynamics. • Define and understand the implications of internal and external politics that impact the discipline. • Value and engage in the intellectual struggle in the discipline. • Function as a producer in the discipline. • Function as a scholar in the discipline.	• Develop awareness of their modes of working as they relate to the modes of operation characteristic of the discipline. • Reflect on the impact of the discipline in the world, and self in the discipline. • Think about the impact of the discipline on the lives of others in the wider world. • Take intellectual samplings of the discipline for the purpose of experiencing self in relation to the discipline. • Examine the ethics and philosophy characteristic of the discipline and their implications. • Project themselves into the discipline • Develop self in the context of the discipline and through interaction with the subject matter. • Develop a sense of both pride and humility related to both self and the discipline.

References

Bateson, M. C. (1989). *Composing a life*. New York: Atlantic Monthly Press.

Bourman, A. (1996). *Meeting of minds*. Portland, ME: Walch.

Connecticut State Department of Education. (1998). *The Connecticut framework: K–12 curricular goals and standards*. Hartford, CT: Author.

Erickson, H. L. (2002). *Concept-based curriculum and instruction: Teaching beyond the facts*. Thousand Oaks, CA: Corwin.

Haseltine, E. (2002, February). The eleven greatest unanswered questions of physics. *Discover: Science, technology and the future*. Retrieved September 19, 2008, from http://discovermagazine.com/2002/feb/cover/

McQuerry, M. (2000). *Nuclear legacy: A collaborative research study with middle school students*. Columbus, OH: Battelle.

Tomlinson, C. A., et al. (2002). *The parallel curriculum: A design to develop high potential and challenge high-ability learners*. Thousand Oaks, CA: Corwin.

Tomlinson, C. A., et al. (2005). *The parallel curriculum in the classroom, book 1: Essays for application across the content areas, K–12*. Thousand Oaks, CA: Corwin.

Tomlinson, C. A., et al. (2008). *The parallel curriculum: A design to develop learner potential and challenge advanced Learners*. Thousand Oaks, CA: Corwin.

U.S. Department of Labor. (1992). *What work requires of schools: A SCANS report for America 2000*. Washington, DC: Government Printing Office.

Wassermann, S. (1988). Play-debrief-replay: An instructional model for science. *Childhood Education, 64*, 232–234.

Wiggins, G., & McTighe, J. (1998). *Understanding by design*. Alexandria, VA: Association for Supervision and Curriculum Development.

Index

CORWIN
A SAGE Company

The Corwin logo—a raven striding across an open book—represents the union of courage and learning. Corwin is committed to improving education for all learners by publishing books and other professional development resources for those serving the field of PreK–12 education. By providing practical, hands-on materials, Corwin continues to carry out the promise of its motto: **"Helping Educators Do Their Work Better."**

MISSION STATEMENT

The National Association for Gifted Children (NAGC) is an organization of parents, teachers, educators, other professionals, and community leaders who unite to address the unique needs of children and youth with demonstrated gifts and talents as well as those children who may be able to develop their talent potential with appropriate educational experiences. We support and develop policies and practices that encourage and respond to the diverse expressions of gifts and talents in children and youth from all cultures, racial and ethnic backgrounds, and socioeconomic groups. NAGC supports and engages in research and development, staff development, advocacy, communication, and collaboration with other organizations and agencies who strive to improve the quality of education for all students.